Wonders

CALIFORNIA Content Reader

English Language Development

A

The McGraw·Hill Companies

Mc Graw Hill Macmillan/McGraw-Hill

Published by Macmillan/McGraw-Hill, of McGraw-Hill Education, a division of The McGraw-Hill Companies, Inc.,
Two Penn Plaza, New York, New York 10121.

Printed in the United States of America

1 2 3 4 5 6 7 8 9 10 073 12 11 10 09 08

Contents

California Science Standards

Contents

Energy

Anything that moves or grows uses energy. Light from the Sun gives Earth most of its energy. Plants take in light to make food and grow. Some animals eat plants. Then the animals get energy from the plants.

Food, batteries, and fuel can store energy. **Fuel** is something that gives off energy when it is burned. Gasoline, coal, and wood are kinds of fuel. Machines use stored energy from fuel to heat buildings. Machines can also change this stored energy into moving energy. This moving energy can make cars go.

Our bodies use the stored energy from food. We use it to move and stay warm. When you run, your body makes heat. Then the stored energy from the food you ate changes into motion and heat.

▲ Light comes from the Sun.

▲ Food gives us energy.

All moving objects have energy. This energy can be carried to other objects. For example, throw a bowling ball. Your moving arm carries energy to the ball. Then the ball carries energy to the pins it hits.

▲ Bowlers use energy to hit pins.

Waves can carry energy from place to place. Waves can move through matter or empty space. Sound waves, light waves, and ocean waves are all kinds of waves.

Energy moves an ocean wave up and down. An ocean wave carries this energy to objects in the water. Sound waves push air back and forth. That's how sound waves carry energy from place to place.

Energy is also carried by an electric current. An electric current comes from power plants. It moves through wires to a socket. When you put a plug into a socket, the current carries energy through the cord. This energy changes into the energy that turns on lamps and computers.

The Future of Energy

One day, more of our energy will come from the Sun, the wind, the ocean, and plants!

Energy from the Sun

Russel Illig/Photodisc/Getty Images

People put special panels on roofs to collect sunlight. These panels take in sunlight. Then the panels turn the sunlight into electrical energy. This energy can heat water and run machines.

Energy from Ocean Waves

Ron Dahlquist/SuperStock

Ocean waves move all day and night. Scientists are changing energy from ocean waves into energy for homes and businesses. Already, people are using energy from ocean waves in Canada and Scotland.

We use energy when we drive cars and turn on lights. Most of our energy comes from burning oil, coal, and gas. Burning fuel pollutes the air. As we use fuel, we have less left. What else can we use for energy?

Wind, plants, sunlight, and ocean waves can give us energy, too. They come from nature. They have clean energy. Even better, we will probably always have them. —*Lisa Jo Rudy*

Energy from Wind

Energy from Plants

Wind farms are groups of windmills. Wind turns the big blades of the windmills. This makes electrical energy. Then this energy can heat water. It can turn on lights and computers.

Some plants can make fuel for cars. This fuel is called biofuel. Sugarcane, corn, and sugar beets are plants that can make this type of clean fuel.

Description Writing Frame

Use the Writing Frame to orally summarize "Energy."

There are many forms of energy. **For example**, _____

_____ .

Energy can **also** be stored in _____

_____ .

Machines can change _____

_____ .

Moving energy can make _____

_____ go.

Our bodies use the stored energy in food. **When** we run, the

stored energy _____

_____ .

Waves can **also** carry energy. _____

_____ are two kinds of waves.

Use the Writing Frame to write the summary on another sheet
of paper. Be sure to include the **bold** signal words. Keep this as
a model of this Text Structure.

Critical Thinking

1 Something that is burned for energy is called _____.

   A. fuel

   B. waves

   C. film

2 Point to the text that names where we get energy in "The Future of Energy."

3 Read aloud the sentences that tell about the energy of wind in "The Future of Energy."

4 Talk about the photographs on pages 8–9 with a partner. How do they help you understand what you have read?

A photograph is a picture taken with a camera.

Digital Learning

For a list of links and activities that relate to this Science standard, visit the California Treasures Web site at www.macmillanmh.com to access the Content Reader resources.

Have students view the Science in Motion video "How You Hear."

In addition, distribute copies of the Translated Concept Summaries in Spanish, Chinese, Hmong, Khmer, and Vietnamese.

Energy and Matter

Matter comes in three forms, or states: solids, liquids, and gases. Each form of matter has certain properties.

Pencils and desks are solids. A **solid** is matter that has a definite shape and volume. Definite means it does not change on its own. **Volume** is the amount of space that an object fills.

▲ The glass is a solid. The milk is a liquid.

A **liquid** has a definite volume, but does not have a definite shape. You can pour a liquid into a container. The liquid takes the shape of the container that holds it. Water, juice, and shampoo are liquids.

A **gas** does not have a definite shape or volume. Most gases are clear and have no color. If you blow gas into a balloon, the gas spreads. It fills the balloon. The gas takes the balloon's shape.

Gas was in the tank. Then the gas filled the balloons. Now the gas takes the shape of the balloons. ▶

Helium

Matter can change. In a **physical change**, matter looks different, but it is still the same matter. In a **chemical change**, matter changes into new matter. The properties of the new matter are different from the properties of the original substances. For example, to make bread dough, combine two things—flour and eggs. Then bake the dough. The baked bread tastes and looks different from the original flour and eggs.

flour and eggs

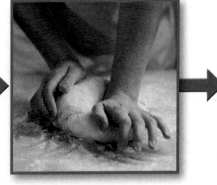
bread dough

baked bread

When you heat matter, it gains heat energy. When matter gains heat energy, it can change its form or state. When a solid gains enough heat energy, it will **melt**. That is it turns into a liquid. Ice cream melts as it gains heat energy. When a liquid gains heat energy, it will **evaporate**. That is, it turns into a gas. If you put wet clothes on a clothesline, the water in the clothes gains heat energy from the Sun. The water evaporates into a gas. The clothes become dry.

▲ Heat energy makes solid steel melt.

Water Troubles

Fresh, clean water is becoming even more precious for millions of people around the world.

Anne Ackermann/Getty Images

▲ In most parts of the U.S., kids play in clean, fresh water.

Water covers about $\frac{3}{4}$ of Earth. However, most water is salty. Very little of Earth's water is fresh water. Much of Earth's fresh water is frozen in ice caps. So, we can use only a tiny part of Earth's fresh water for washing, drinking, cooking, and watering plants.

We usually have enough clean, fresh water in the United States. We turn on a faucet and there it is. Many parts of Africa, Asia, and Latin America do not have enough fresh water.

Why don't some places have enough water? In some places, people use water from wells. People use the water faster than rain can refill the wells. Many places have droughts. A drought is a long time without enough rain. Also, water turns to gas when the Sun shines on it. The gas rises up into the air. Then the water is gone. The ground becomes dry. No plants can grow.

Rao Guojun/ChinaFotoPress/Getty

▲ In some countries, there's no water to spare.

It is not safe to drink all fresh water. Water in wells, lakes, and rivers may contain tiny living things that can make you sick. Chemicals can make water unsafe.

We can solve water problems. Kids and adults can learn how to protect water and use it wisely.

▲ A boy drinks water from a lake in the country of Mali in Africa.

Clean Water for School

One school in Romania had old water pipes. Dirty water came out of them. The school children drank the dirty water. They washed their hands with it. Children got sick. A Romanian aid group and the Earth Day Network put new water pipes in the school. Now the school has fresh, clean water. —*Kathryn Satterfield*

Kids Help!

Three teenagers solved a water problem and won a prize!

▲ The winners!

Pontso Moletsane, Motobele Motschodi, and Sechaba Ramabenyane grew up in South Africa. Together, they found a way to water crops using less water. They made a watering system that works at night. Since the Sun does not shine at night, less water dries up then. The new system will help South Africa save water.

Compare/Contrast Writing Frame

Use the Writing Frame to orally summarize "Energy and Matter."

Solids, liquids and gases are **all** _____

_____ .

A solid and a liquid **both** have a definite _____ .

Unlike a solid, a liquid does not have a definite _____

_____ .

A gas is **different** from a solid because _____

_____

_____ .

Solids are **similar** to liquids because they can change. When a

solid gains heat energy, it may _____ .

Liquids are **different** from solids. When liquids gain heat energy,

they can _____ .

So, _____ are the **same** and also
are **different**.

Use the Writing Frame to write the summary on another sheet of
paper. Be sure to include the **bold** signal words. Keep this as a
model of this Text Structure.

Critical Thinking

1. The amount of space that an object fills is called _____.

   A. volume

   B. evaporation

   C. solid

2. Point out the sentences in "Energy and Matter" that compare and contrast a physical change with a chemical change.

3. Read aloud the text that tells what happens to a liquid when it evaporates.

4. Describe for a partner what the three arrows in the middle of page 13 show.

Arrows can show how things change. They show how one step follows another.

Digital Learning

For a list of links and activities that relate to this Science standard, visit the California Treasures Web site at www.macmillanmh.com to access the Content Reader resources.

Have students view the Science in Motion video "From Solid to Liquid to Gas."

In addition, distribute copies of the Translated Concept Summaries in Spanish, Chinese, Hmong, Khmer, and Vietnamese.

Science

Elements and Atoms

Long ago people thought that all matter was made from earth, wind, fire, and water.

Today scientists use experiments and special microscopes to look at matter. Now we know that all matter is made up of **elements**. The **periodic table** lists the known elements. More than 100 of these elements have names. Some elements are named after places. *Californium* is named for California.

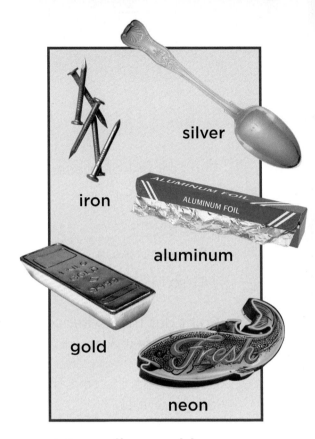

▲ Iron, silver, gold, aluminum, and neon are elements in these objects.

The Periodic Table of the Elements

Key

- 11 —Atomic number
- Na —Element symbol
- Sodium —Element name
- ☐ Metals
- ☐ Metalloids (semimetals)
- ☐ Nonmetals

1												13	14	15	16	17	18
1 **H** Hydrogen	2																2 **He** Helium
3 **Li** Lithium	4 **Be** Beryllium	3	4	5	6	7	8	9	10	11	12	5 **B** Boron	6 **C** Carbon	7 **N** Nitrogen	8 **O** Oxygen	9 **F** Fluorine	10 **Ne** Neon
11 **Na** Sodium	12 **Mg** Magnesium											13 **Al** Aluminum	14 **Si** Silicon	15 **P** Phosphorus	16 **S** Sulfur	17 **Cl** Chlorine	18 **Ar** Argon
19 **K** Potassium	20 **Ca** Calcium	21 **Sc** Scandium	22 **Ti** Titanium	23 **V** Vanadium	24 **Cr** Chromium	25 **Mn** Manganese	26 **Fe** Iron	27 **Co** Cobalt	28 **Ni** Nickel	29 **Cu** Copper	30 **Zn** Zinc	31 **Ga** Gallium	32 **Ge** Germanium	33 **As** Arsenic	34 **Se** Selenium	35 **Br** Bromine	36 **Kr** Krypton
37 **Rb** Rubidium	38 **Sr** Strontium	39 **Y** Yttrium	40 **Zr** Zirconium	41 **Nb** Niobium	42 **Mo** Molybdenum	43 **Tc** Technetium	44 **Ru** Ruthenium	45 **Rh** Rhodium	46 **Pd** Palladium	47 **Ag** Silver	48 **Cd** Cadmium	49 **In** Indium	50 **Sn** Tin	51 **Sb** Antimony	52 **Te** Tellurium	53 **I** Iodine	54 **Xe** Xenon
55 **Cs** Cesium	56 **Ba** Barium	57 **La** Lanthanum	72 **Hf** Hafnium	73 **Ta** Tantalum	74 **W** Tungsten	75 **Re** Rhenium	76 **Os** Osmium	77 **Ir** Iridium	78 **Pt** Platinum	79 **Au** Gold	80 **Hg** Mercury	81 **Tl** Thallium	82 **Pb** Lead	83 **Bi** Bismuth	84 **Po** Polonium	85 **At** Astatine	86 **Rn** Radon
87 **Fr** Francium	88 **Ra** Radium	89 **Ac** Actinium	104 **Rf** Rutherfordium	105 **Db** Dubnium	106 **Sg** Seaborgium	107 **Bh** Bohrium	108 **Hs** Hassium	109 **Mt** Meitnerium	110 **Ds** Darmstadtium	111 **Rg** Roentgenium	**Uub** Ununbium						

58 **Ce** Cerium	59 **Pr** Praseodymium	60 **Nd** Neodymium	61 **Pm** Promethium	62 **Sm** Samarium	63 **Eu** Europium	64 **Gd** Gadolinium	65 **Tb** Terbium	66 **Dy** Dysprosium	67 **Ho** Holmium	68 **Er** Erbium	69 **Tm** Thulium	70 **Yb** Ytterbium	71 **Lu** Lutetium
90 **Th** Thorium	91 **Pa** Protactinium	92 **U** Uranium	93 **Np** Neptunium	94 **Pu** Plutonium	95 **Am** Americium	96 **Cm** Curium	97 **Bk** Berkelium	98 **Cf** Californium	99 **Es** Einsteinium	100 **Fm** Fermium	101 **Md** Mendelevium	102 **No** Nobelium	103 **Lr** Lawrencium

Elements are made up of tiny particles called atoms. An **atom** is the smallest unit of an element that has the same properties as the element. All the atoms of one element are identical.

Atoms are everywhere. But you cannot see atoms with just your eye. You cannot even see atoms with most microscopes. Scientists study atoms with special *electron microscopes*. Electron microscopes are very powerful.

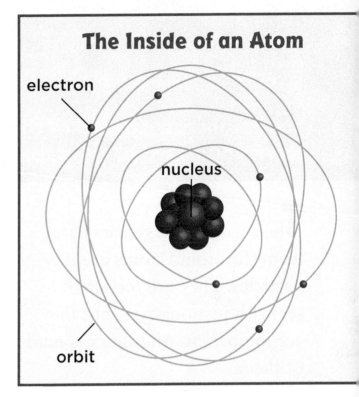

The Inside of an Atom

electron

nucleus

orbit

Atoms are very tiny. Atoms are much smaller than apples. Apples are much smaller than Earth. ▼

The Atomic Age

You might have heard of the Ice Age. Have you heard of the Atomic Age?

The Atomic Age gets its name from the atom. Atoms are tiny particles. They are too small to see with just our eyes, but they are important. All matter is made of them.

At the end of the nineteenth century, scientists discovered that atoms can change. Atoms give off energy when they change. This energy is called atomic energy.

The Beginning of the Atomic Age

Most people say the Atomic Age started in the late 1930s. This is when scientists found out how to get energy from atoms. Soon after, scientists learned how to use atomic energy to make bombs.

An important year in the Atomic Age was 1946. During World War II, the United States dropped two atomic bombs on Japan. Thousands of people were killed instantly. Thousands more died later. World War II soon ended.

▲ An atomic bomb exploded in Japan.

Using Atomic Energy for Peaceful Purposes

It was the 1950s. Atomic energy was also called nuclear energy. Scientists discovered that nuclear energy could be used to make electricity. Doctors could use it to help sick people.

The Ford Motor Company wanted to make a car that used atomic energy. In 1957 Ford showed a model of a car that used atomic energy. This car was called the Nucleon. The Nucleon was never built. It was not practical.

▼ This power plant uses nuclear energy.

The Atomic Age ended in the 1960s. Nuclear energy was still used to make electricity. However, many people did not think nuclear energy was safe.

The Future

Nuclear energy is part of modern life. Scientists are still trying to use it safely to make clean energy. Maybe another Atomic Age will happen soon.

▼ The Nucleon was not made.

Bettmann/Corbis

Peter Widmann/Alamy

21

Problem/Solution Writing Frame

**Use the Writing Frame to orally summarize
"Elements and Atoms."**

Long ago people did not know what made matter.

To **solve their problem**, they thought that all matter was _____

_____ .

Today, scientists have **solved** the same **problem**. They use _____

_____ .

As a result, scientists now know that all matter is _____

_____ .

Without special microscopes, scientists would not know that
matter is made up of elements. This is **because** elements are

made up of _____ .

Atoms are everywhere, but the **problem** is that _____

_____ .

As a result, scientists _____

_____ .

Use the Writing Frame to write the summary on another sheet
of paper. Be sure to include the **bold** signal words. Keep this as
a model of this Text Structure.

Critical Thinking

1 All matter is made up of _____.

    A. microscopes

    B. experiments

    C. elements

2 Look at "Elements and Atoms" on page 18. Show a partner where to find the sentence that tells how many elements have been named.

3 Revisit page 19. Read aloud the text that tells about electron microscopes.

4 Describe the table on page 18 to a partner.

A table shows a lot of information, such as names and numbers, in a way that uses less space.

Digital Learning

For a list of links and activities that relate to this Science standard, visit the California Treasures Web site at www.macmillanmh.com to access the Content Reader resources.

Have students view the e-Review "Building Blocks of Matter."

In addition, distribute copies of the Translated Concept Summaries in Spanish, Chinese, Hmong, Khmer, and Vietnamese.

Science

Shadows

How do you stay dry on a rainy day? You stand under an umbrella. Rain slides down the umbrella's sides. Since the raindrops do not pass through the umbrella, the rain does not touch you.

Opaque materials act like an umbrella. When light energy hits **opaque** materials, they absorb some of it. They reflect some light energy, too. This is how opaque objects block light energy from passing through them. When light is blocked, a shadow forms. A **shadow** is a dark space.

▼ Rain does not pass through the umbrella.

A dog, a tree, and a person are opaque objects. They do not let light pass through. Opaque objects make shadows. The shadows form on the opposite side of the light source.

Opaque materials do not let you see the objects behind them. Remember, you see an object when light reflects from the object and enters your eyes. Opaque materials block light. Then you cannot see the object.

▲ Shadows always form on the opposite side of a light source.

◀ Opaque objects block or stop light from passing through them. This causes shadows.

Sunlight and Shadow

For thousands of years, the Sun has played an important part in where—and how—buildings are built.

People who design buildings need to understand sunlight and shadow.

The Sun and Stonehenge

Stonehenge is an ancient circle of big stones in England. No one knows who built Stonehenge or why these stones were placed there. However, on the first official day of summer (the summer solstice), sunrise happens behind one of the biggest stones. Minutes later the Sun looks like a ball of fire on top of the stone.

Whoever built Stonehenge knew about sunrise. They knew about light and shadow.

Right after sunrise, the Sun is over Stonehenge on the summer solstice.

Bill Bachmann/Photo Researchers, Inc.

Sunshine in Your Bedroom

The builders of Stonehenge were like modern architects. Architects are people who design buildings. They design houses, parks, and factories. Architects think about light and shadow for their designs.

Architects know about sunrise and sunset. So they must think about light and shadow. For example, architects can build a bedroom that faces east to get morning light. They can make a living room face west in the direction of sunset.

Architects design houses to fit into a neighborhood. They design skyscrapers to fit into a city. First, they build models to see if their new building will fit well into a place. The models show if the new building will block someone else's light. Architects can also see if existing buildings and hills will make the new building too dark.

Computers help architects build models. Sometimes architects build models from cardboard and wood. The models help architects figure out how to place their buildings to get the most from the Sun. —*Lisa Jo Rudy*

▼ Architects make models to show how sunlight and shadow affect buildings.

Li Jiangsong/Imaginechina/Zuma Press/Newscom

27

Cause/Effect Writing Frame

Use the Writing Frame to orally summarize "Sunlight and Shadow."

Everyone who designs buildings needs to understand the **effect** of sunlight and shadow.

Sunrise takes place behind one of the biggest stones of

Stonehenge on _____

_____.

The **effect** of this is that the Sun _____

_____.

Because of the **effect** of sunrise and sunset, architects must _____

_____.

Architects build models to see _____

_____.

The **effect** of this is that architects must figure out _____

_____.

Use the Writing Frame to write the summary on another sheet of paper. Be sure to include the **bold** signal words. Keep this as a model of this Text Structure.

Critical Thinking

1. If a material can absorb some light energy, it is _____.

   A. opaque

   B. object

   C. rainy

2. Find the words in "Shadows" that define a shadow.

3. Point to the paragraph in "Shadows" about umbrellas. How are opaque materials like an umbrella?

4. With a partner, find the photographs on page 25 that show shadows. Read each caption aloud.

A caption is an explanation of a photograph.

Digital Learning

For a list of links and activities that relate to this Science standard, visit the California Treasures Web site at www.macmillanmh.com to access the Content Reader resources.

Have students view the e-Review "Shadows."

In addition, distribute copies of the Translated Concept Summaries in Spanish, Chinese, Hmong, Khmer, and Vietnamese.

Light and Color

A ball hits the ground and bounces up. Light acts much like this ball. When light hits an object, it bounces off in a new direction. Then it moves in a straight path. When light waves bounce off an object it is called **reflection**.

▲ Light is like a ball that bounces.

A mirror is a smooth, shiny surface. Smooth, shiny surfaces reflect almost all light that hits them. This is because light bounces off smooth surfaces in one direction. Then a clear picture can form. Light bounces off rough surfaces in different directions. Then a clear picture cannot form.

When light hits a smooth pond, the image on the pond's surface is clear.

The leaf
looks green.

The flower
looks red.

White light is made of seven different colors of light. White light can hit an object. Then some colors of light are **absorbed**, or taken in. Other colors of light are reflected. When you look at the object, some of the reflected light enters your eyes. You see the object as the color of the reflected light.

White light that hits a leaf is made of seven different colors. The leaf absorbs all the colors except green. The green light bounces off the leaf. It is reflected to your eyes. So you see the leaf as green. When white light hits a red flower, only red light is reflected. All the other colors are absorbed. So you see the flower as red.

Searching the Skies

Richard Wainscoat/Alamy

The Keck telescopes have mirrors that are 32 feet across.

Mirrors and computers help us solve some of the mysteries of the universe.

How far can humans see into outer space? It depends on how powerful our telescopes are.

Many telescopes have mirrors inside them. The mirrors collect light. A telescope's power depends on the size of its mirror. An enormous, perfect mirror can capture the light of a star far away. The most powerful optical (or light-collecting) telescopes are the two Keck telescopes on Mount Mauna Kea in Hawaii. These telescopes have discovered new planets very far away. Each telescope has a mirror that is 32 feet across.

Telescopes used to be difficult to make. They were very expensive and heavy. Then, in the 1980s, scientists invented ways to make bigger, lighter mirrors. Jerry Nelson, a California astronomer, designed the Keck's mirror. Nelson used 36 small sheets of glass instead of one big sheet. A computer makes the 36 sheets move together as one.

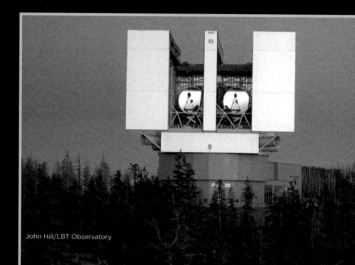

John Hill/LBT Observatory

In 2004, scientists began to build an even more powerful telescope in Arizona. The Large Binocular Telescope (LBT) will be able to look far into space.

LBT will combine light from two enormous mirrors. In October 2005, LBT took its first picture of space using just one mirror. —*Lisa Jo Rudy*

◀ Seeing even deeper into the universe: the Large Binocular Telescope in Arizona

How Mirrors Collect Light

The first telescopes used glass lenses to collect light. But these telescopes had a problem. They broke the light from the stars into a rainbow. This made it hard to see clearly. Isaac Newton, an English scientist, decided to try using a mirror inside a telescope instead.

▲ **Isaac Newton's telescope**

In 1680, Newton built his first reflecting telescope. He used a curved, metal mirror to collect light from stars. The mirror also reflected the light to a focus. A focus is the place where you put your eye to see the light.

Today, we still use Newton's design for the reflecting telescope. Small, ordinary telescopes use new types of mirrors. You can see the craters of the Moon with an ordinary telescope. You can see the stars, and the rings of Saturn, too.

NASA

33

Description Writing Frame

**Use the Writing Frame to orally summarize
"Seeing Light and Color."**

Light **has interesting characteristics**. It acts _____

_____ .

When light hits an object, _____

_____ .

White light is made up of _____

_____ .

When white light hits an object, some colors of light _____

_____ .

When white light hits a leaf, _____

_____ .

But when white light hits a red flower, _____

_____ .

Use the Writing Frame to write the summary on another sheet
of paper. Be sure to include the **bold** signal words. Keep this as
a model of this Text Structure.

Critical Thinking

1 When a color of light is taken in, it is ———————.

    A. smooth

    B. bounced

    C. absorbed

2 Point to the sentence in "Searching the Skies" on page 32 that tells what the power of a telescope depends on.

3 Find the sentences in this article that tell about Keck's mirror.

4 What do the diagrams in the photographs on page 31 tell you? Discuss this with a partner.

A diagram is a drawing or a plan. It explains how something works.

Digital Learning

For a list of links and activities that relate to this Science standard, visit the California Treasures Web site at www.macmillanmh.com to access the Content Reader resources.

Have students view the Science in Motion video "Seeing Colors." In addition, distribute copies of the Translated Concept Summaries in Spanish, Chinese, Hmong, Khmer, and Vietnamese.

Plants and Their Needs

Most plants have the same basic needs. They need water, sunlight, energy from food, and carbon dioxide. Carbon dioxide is a gas found in air. Plants need nutrients, too. Nutrients are substances that help living things grow and stay healthy. Plants must get all these things from their environment. These things enable plants to survive.

Stems carry food and water through the plant. Stems also help a plant stand up. Then its leaves can get sunlight.

Roots take in water and nutrients from the soil. They keep a plant in place.

Plants have structures that help them get or make things they need. A **structure** is a part of a living thing. Most plants have roots, stems, and leaves. These parts help a plant to get what it needs to make its own food.

Many plants also have flowers, fruits, and seeds. These parts help plants live, grow, and reproduce. *Reproduce* means to make new plants like themselves.

Leaves take in carbon dioxide from the air. They use energy from the Sun to change carbon dioxide and water into food for the plant.

This Flower Stinks!

Thousands of people went to the Brooklyn Botanic Garden in New York. They wanted to see a rare flower called a titan arum. The titan arum grows naturally in the country of Indonesia. The enormous plant is over five and a half feet tall!

However, the flowers of the titan arum smell terrible. They smell like a dead animal. That is why many people call the plant another name: corpse flower!

The titan arum's flower smells terrible. ▶

A Big Baby

The gardeners at the Brooklyn Botanic Garden call their titan arum Baby. Baby grew in Brooklyn for ten years. It had never bloomed, or made a flower. Finally, it did. It was the first titan arum to bloom in New York City since 1939.

Baby grew more than 30 inches in 9 days before it bloomed. Some flowers can grow to nine feet tall! Scientists knew that Baby was ready to open when it stopped growing. The flower took two hours to open. Then out came the smell!

In nature, the titan arum's smell attracts beetles and bees. Its pollen sticks to their legs and bodies. The insects carry the pollen when they fly to other plants. Plants need pollen from other plants of the same kind. Then they can produce more plants of that kind.

People can smell the titan arum from a half mile away. Still, this big plant is in trouble. Some people in Indonesia dig them up. They want to sell them. This is not legal. Also, some people are destroying the forest where the titan arum lives.

▲ The titan arum's home is destroyed.

Problem/Solution Writing Frame

Use the Writing Frame to orally summarize "Plants and Their Needs"

Most plants have the same basic needs. **Problems** begin when

these plants do not get _____.

Plants would also have a problem without nutrients **because**

_____.

But plants have structures that help them avoid **problems**. The

roots of a plant _____

_____.

The stems of plants _____

_____.

The leaves of plants _____

_____.

To grow and reproduce, many plants have _____

_____.

Use the Writing Frame to write the summary on another sheet of paper. Be sure to include the **bold** signal word. Keep this as a model of this Text Structure.

Critical Thinking

1 A part of a living thing is called a _____.

    A. structure

    B. environment

    C. sunlight

2 Read "This Flower Stinks!" Find the description of the titan arum. Discuss this with a partner.

3 Read "This Flower Stinks!" Point out the sentences that tell how Baby is different from most plants.

4 Use the captions on pages 36 and 37 to show a partner how plants get what they need.

A caption explains what is shown in a picture.

Digital Learning

For a list of links and activities that relate to this Science standard, visit the California Treasures Web site at www.macmillanmh.com to access the Content Reader resources.

Have students view the Science e-Review "Living Things and Their Needs."

In addition, distribute copies of the Translated Concept Summaries in Spanish, Chinese, Hmong, Khmer, and Vietnamese.

Animals and Their Needs

All animals have the same basic needs. Animals need water, energy from food, and oxygen. Oxygen is a gas in air and water. Animals need shelter and safety, too. A **shelter** is a place where animals can stay safe.

Animals have structures that help them get things they need. Legs, wings, and beaks are examples of animal structures.

▲ Birds use nests for shelter.

Food, Water, and Oxygen

Animals cannot make their own food the way plants can. They must eat plants or other animals. Legs, fins, and wings help animals move to find food. Beaks and tongues help animals catch and swallow food. Beaks and tongues help animals drink water, too.

A lion's tongue helps it get water. ▶

Structures help animals get oxygen. To get oxygen, many animals breathe with lungs. Lungs take in oxygen from the air. Fish have gills to take in oxygen. They push water through them. The gills take in oxygen from the water.

▲ Gills help fish get oxygen.

Shelter and Safety

Some animals use trees or other plants for shelter. Other animals build shelters. Birds build nests as shelters for their babies. Birds use their beaks and feet to get materials and build nests.

Some animals have structures that help them stay safe. A kangaroo's pouch helps baby kangaroos stay safe. A porcupine has sharp quills. The quills help it stay safe from other animals.

A baby kangaroo grows in its mother's pouch. It stays safe. ▶

Meerkats

Meerkats survive in Africa's Kalahari Desert by working together.

Meerkats live in the Kalahari Desert in Africa. Life is hard there. Other animals try to eat them.

Meerkats are little, furry animals. They are only one foot long. They are not very strong.

Meerkats survive by working together. They help each other find food. They help raise children and protect each other, too.

▲ A meerkat eats lunch!

A Mob

Up to 30 meerkats can live together in a group. This group is called a mob. Each mob lives in its own area. The mob builds a burrow in the desert sand. The mob looks for food and water, too.

This is a mob of meerkats.

Meerkats leave their safe burrow during the day. They look for food in the sand. They dig out beetles and scorpions with their strong feet and claws.

Everyone Shares

Meerkats find food by working together. Each day, one meerkat is the lookout for the group. The lookout stands up on its two hind legs. Then it looks for animals that may attack. Now the other meerkats can hunt safely. If the lookout sees danger, it barks loudly. This bark is the signal to run away. Then the meerkats hide in the nearest burrow. Sometimes they cannot escape. Then the meerkats, working together, scare their enemy away.

Meerkats stay close together at night. They hug each other before they sleep. —*Curtis Slepian*

A Meerkat's Body

A meerkat is only two pounds. Its body enables it to survive.

Nigel J. Dennis; Gallo Images/CORBIS

Eyes — It has powerful eyes. It can see enemies from far away.

Ears — It can close its ears. This keeps out desert sand.

Nose — It has a strong sense of smell. This helps it find insects in the sand.

Fur — The brown color helps it blend in with sand and rocks.

Tail — It uses its tail as a third leg. This helps it balance.

Feet — It has powerful front claws. It can dig up hundreds of pounds of sand each day.

45

Problem/Solution Writing Frame

**Use the Writing Frame to orally summarize
"Animals and Their Needs."**

All animals have the same basic needs. **Problems** begin when

animals do not get _____ .

To help **solve the problem** of getting things they need, animals

have _____ .

One **problem** that animals have is that they cannot make

_____ .

Animals must _____

_____ .

Another problem most animals have is that they need _____

_____ .

Some animals **solve** this **problem** by using _____

_____ .

Other animals build _____ .

Use the Writing Frame to write the summary on another sheet
of paper. Be sure to include the **bold** signal word. Keep this as a
model of this Text Structure.

Critical Thinking

1   A place where animals can stay safe is called a _____.

   A. shelter

   B. oxygen

   C. quills

2   Read the sentences in "Meerkats" that describe this animal. Discuss them with a partner.

3   Point out the sentence in "Meerkats" that tells what meerkats do before they sleep.

4   Find the label in the photograph of the fish on page 43. Discuss the label with a partner.

A label points something out in a picture.

Digital Learning

For a list of links and activities that relate to this Science standard, visit the California Treasures Web site at www.macmillanmh.com to access the Content Reader resources.

Have students view the e-Review "Living Things and Their Needs." In addition, distribute copies of the Translated Concept Summaries in Spanish, Chinese, Hmong, Khmer, and Vietnamese.

Science

Living Things in Different Environments

An **adaptation** is a body part or way of acting that helps a living thing survive in its environment.

Arctic tundra plants have adaptations such as shallow roots. These roots help them survive in frozen soil. Most arctic plants grow close to the ground. This protects them from cold and wind.

Many forest trees grow tall. This is an adaptation. The trees grow toward light. Plants on the forest floor may have large leaves. This helps them take in as much light as possible.

Plants in wetland areas have tubes in their stems. These tubes carry oxygen from their leaves to their roots.

Most grassland grasses have adaptations to grow in dry conditions. Their deep roots drink up water.

Algae live in the ocean. They are like plants, but have no roots. This adaptation permits them to float near the sunlit surface of the water.

▲ This desert plant has waxy skin and thick leaves to help it store water in a dry environment.

Grasses and reeds grow in wetlands. ▶

Animals have adaptations, too. For example, many desert animals come out only at night when it is cooler. Many have ways of staying cool.

Wetland animals have adaptations to live in water. Some breathe through their skin. Many ocean animals have gills. Gills take in oxygen from water.

Many arctic tundra animals have thick fur coats and a layer of fat. The fur and fat keep them warm. Others have wide, furry feet. These feet help them run on snow.

Some grassland animals have flat teeth to eat grasses. Small animals have adaptations to help them hide.

Seasons change in forests. Animals in forests may eat extra food. They may grow thicker coats that keep them warm. They may go into a deep sleep during winter.

▲ Zebras use their flat teeth to bite grass.

 Water enters the fish's mouth.

❷ The gills take in oxygen from the water.

A Whole New World!

Scientists discover unknown animals on land and in the sea.

This fish was unknown before.

Under the Sea

Scientists have discovered fish that change color very fast. They also found sharks that can walk. These animals live in part of the Indian Ocean. This area is near the coast of Papua New Guinea, in Indonesia.

A group called Conservation International sent 12 scientists to the area. The scientists identified 24 new kinds of fish, 20 kinds of coral, and 8 kinds of shrimp. This happened in six weeks!

Two types of epaulette sharks were discovered. Epaulette sharks are three feet long and have spots. They live in shallow water. They can use their fins to walk on the ocean floor!

This shark can walk! ▼

AP Photo/World Wildlife Fund Indonesia, Wahyu Gumelar, HO

▲ Scientists think the mysterious animal looks like this.

New Creatures on Land

Scientists are also making new discoveries on land. A team from the World Wildlife Fund (WWF) may have found an unknown animal in the rain forests of Borneo. Borneo is a large island. It is divided among the countries of Malaysia, Indonesia, and Brunei.

The mysterious creature looks like a cat and a fox. It has dark red fur and a long, bushy tail. It has small ears and large hind, or back, legs. Researchers took two photographs of the animal.

Stephan Wulffraat is a biologist. He and his team consulted with wildlife experts in Borneo. Some experts thought the animal looked like a lemur. Most experts thought this is an animal that eats other animals. Wulffraat said they cannot be sure what the animal is until they capture one live.

The WWF must find the animal fast. Its home may be destroyed. A palm oil plantation may be built in the rain forest where the animal was photographed. —*Claudia Atticot*

51

Cause/Effect Writing Frame

**Use the Writing Frame to orally summarize
"Living Things in Different Environments."**

An adaptation helps a living thing survive in its environment.

Some desert plants have thick leaves. The **effect** is that the

plants can _____.

Arctic tundra plants can survive in frozen soil **because** _____

_____.

If a tree in the forest grows tall, **then** it has an adaptation to

grow toward _____.

If grasses grow deep roots that drink up water, **then** they have

an adaptation to _____.

Some animals can live in the wetlands **because** they have _____

_____.

Therefore, the **effect** of adaptation is _____

_____.

Use the Writing Frame to write the summary on another sheet
of paper. Be sure to include the **bold** signal word. Keep this as a
model of this Text Structure.

Critical Thinking

1 Living things that are like plants and float in the ocean are called _____.

    A. animals

    B. adaptations

    C. algae

2 Point out where in "A Whole New World!" the text describes epaulette sharks.

3 Read aloud the sentences in "A Whole New World!" that tell about a mysterious kind of animal on Borneo.

4 Describe for a partner what the numbers in the photograph on page 49 show.

Numbers show how one step follows another.

Digital Learning

For a list of links and activities that relate to this Science standard, visit the California Treasures Web site at www.macmillanmh.com to access the Content Reader resources.

Have students view the Science in Motion video "Adaptations of Desert Plants."

In addition, distribute copies of the Translated Concept Summaries in Spanish, Chinese, Hmong, Khmer, and Vietnamese.

Living Things Change Their Environments

Every living thing changes its environment in some way. A spider spins a web. A bird builds a nest. A squirrel buries an acorn. All these actions change the environment in small ways.

Living things can also change their environments in bigger ways. Bacteria, worms, and fungi live in the soil. They break down leaves and other dead plant material. They help add nutrients back to the soil. These living things change and help the environment.

Competition can be a major cause of change. **Competition** is the struggle among living things for food, water, and other needs.

Grass and other small plants sprout in warm, wet soil. They change this environment as they grow.

More plants grow. Other living things move to the environment. These living things use the plants for food and shelter.

When grass grows, it takes in nutrients and water from the soil. It changes the environment as it gets things it needs. Animals eat the grass for food. These animals change the environment as they get what they need. In time, larger plants such as shrubs and trees grow. They compete for space, light, and water. The trees block sunlight from the smaller plants. The smaller plants may die. This is how environments change as living things compete to get what they need.

When shrubs grow, more animals move to the environment. The plants and animals compete as they get what they need.

In time, trees grow. The environment continues to change.

Gone!

Extinction can be a natural process. It can also be caused by human actions.

Eighty kinds of birds have become extinct in the last 300 years. Some died out from natural causes. Others became extinct because people destroyed their habitat.

Read the stories of two extinct birds. They can teach us how people can protect other living things.

◀ The dodo bird is extinct.

The Dodo

Sailors first saw dodos around 1600 on the island of Mauritius in the Indian Ocean. The fat dodos were the perfect food for the sailors and their animals. The birds could not fly. They were easy to catch. People also cut down much of the forests on the island. They wanted the wood from the trees. So, the dodos lost their home and source of food. About 80 years after the sailors arrived, the dodo was extinct.

Photo Researchers

◀ The Carolina parakeet is extinct.

The Carolina Parakeet

This bird was the only parrot native to the eastern United States. Once, many Carolina parakeets lived in the southeastern United States. They ate fruit. So farmers thought they were hungry pests. People hunted the birds for their beautiful feathers, too. These parrots became extinct in the 1920s. —*Lisa Jo Rudy*

Steven Holt-Courtesy of ANSP/Picturedesk International/Newscom

wolverine

fl online/Alamy

Endangered Plants and Animals in California

There are hundreds of threatened and endangered plants and animals in California. When living things are labeled "threatened" or "endangered," the government may protect them. Then, people can't hunt them or harm them.

Here are some endangered animals in California:

- sea lion
- sperm whale
- wolverine
- sea otter
- California condor
- northern spotted owl

- California pelican
- green, loggerhead, leatherback, and olive ridley sea turtles
- desert tortoise

Richard Mittleman/
Gon2Foto/Alamy

California condor

57

Sequence Writing Frame

**Use the Writing Frame to orally summarize
"Living Things Change Their Environments"**

Every living thing changes its environment.

Bacteria, worms, and fungi break down _____

_____ .

Because of what they do, they help add _____

_____ .

At the **same time** that grass grows, _____

_____ .

Then animals _____ .

As large plants and trees grow, they block _____ .

Then, the smaller plants _____

_____ .

Use the Writing Frame to write the summary on another sheet
of paper. Be sure to include the **bold** signal word. Keep this as a
model of this Text Structure.

Critical Thinking

1 The struggle among living things for food, water, and other needs is called _____.

    A. competition

    B. change

    C. nutrients

2 Reread the paragraph in "Gone!" that tells about dodo birds. Discuss it with a partner.

3 Show a partner which paragraph in "Gone!" tells about a bird that became extinct in the 1920s.

4 Use the list on page 57 to talk about endangered animals in California.

A list is a series of items put in a meaningful grouping.

Digital Learning

For a list of links and activities that relate to this Science standard, visit the California Treasures Website at www.macmillanmh.com to access the Content Reader resources.

Have students view the Science in Motion video, "A Changing Environment."

In addition, distribute copies of the Translated Concept Summaries in Spanish, Chinese, Hmong, Khmer, and Vietnamese.

Science

Changes Affect Plants

When an environment changes, its plants can be harmed. Some plants have adaptations that help them survive. Others may survive by changing how they live. Living things that cannot change may die.

Living things can change their environment. Weather can also change environments. Lightning may start a grassland or forest fire. Too much rain may cause a flood.

These are wildflowers in Anza Borrego State Park, California. They bloom quickly after a spring rain.

▲ Mount St. Helens, a volcano in Washington, erupted in 1980. This eruption knocked down or burnt trees on 230 square miles of forest. The environment is changing as new plants grow.

Some changes last a short time. A summer **drought**, or period of dry weather, can make a green meadow turn brown. Spring rain can make a desert bloom with flowers. Earthquakes, storms, and volcanic eruptions can cause sudden changes in an environment. This damage can last for years.

Some living things can recover from harmful changes in their environment. Grassland grasses have roots that store food and water. The grasses survive. They grow back quickly after a fire. However, trees take years to grow back after a fire.

People may cause permanent changes. Sometimes they cut down large trees in old forests. Then those trees are gone forever. Sometimes trash pollutes rivers and lakes. They may not recover unless people clean them up.

The Heat Is On!

How may global warming affect crops and other living things?

Earth's temperatures have changed naturally in the past. Long ago, the Ice Age was caused naturally. Now, there is evidence that humans are also causing a change—global warming.

Human-made Changes?

An atmosphere surrounds Earth. It is made of air and other gases. This atmosphere works like a glass greenhouse. It naturally traps heat from the Sun. This is why the air inside a greenhouse is warm when the temperature is cool outside. This "greenhouse effect" makes life possible on Earth.

Earth can get too hot if there is too much greenhouse gas. We add greenhouse gases to the atmosphere when we burn fuels, such as coal and oil. Kevin Trenberth of the National Center for Atmospheric Research says, "We are already seeing fewer frost days, heavier rains, and more droughts and heat waves."

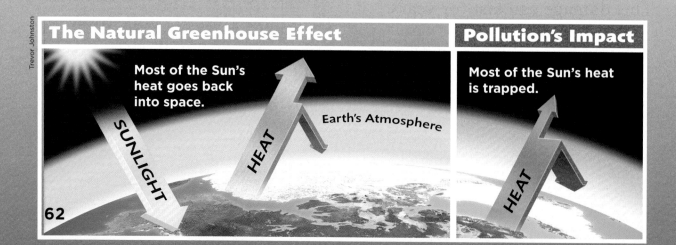

The Natural Greenhouse Effect

Most of the Sun's heat goes back into space.

SUNLIGHT

HEAT

Earth's Atmosphere

Pollution's Impact

Most of the Sun's heat is trapped.

HEAT

What Can Happen to Plants?

Hotter temperatures may affect where important crops, such as wheat and corn, grow. In some areas, such as Canada and Russia, warmer weather may permit longer growing seasons. There may be better harvests. In other areas, such as the southern United States, the weather may be too hot. Harvests may be small. Crops can also suffer if there is too much rain. Winds from strong storms can damage plants, too.

▲ A healthy cornfield.

What Can Happen to Animals?

Warmer waters can cause problems. Seals and seabirds may have trouble finding cold-water food called krill. Ice sheets that melt at the North and South Poles may add more water to the oceans. The oceans may rise. They could flood coasts and islands where people live.

What Can We Do?

We can reduce greenhouse gases to help slow global warming. Some countries have agreed to do this. They signed a treaty called the Kyoto Protocol. In time, other countries may join them. —*David Bjerklie*

▲ Higher temperatures damaged this corn.

Cause/Effect Writing Frame

**Use the Writing Frame to orally summarize
"Changes Affect Plants."**

When an environment changes, its plants can be harmed.

Weather can **affect** plants. Lightning may **cause** _____

_____.

Too much rain can **cause** _____

_____.

A period of dry weather can **cause** _____

_____.

A spring rain can **cause** _____.

People can **cause** permanent changes. When large trees are cut

down, _____

_____.

Therefore, the **effect** of change _____

_____.

Use the Writing Frame to write the summary on another sheet
of paper. Be sure to include the **bold** signal word. Keep this as a
model of this Text Structure.

Critical Thinking

1 A period of dry weather is called a _____.

   A. fire

   B. drought

   C. desert

2 Find the sentence in "Changes Affect Plants" that names three things that cause sudden changes. Discuss it with a partner.

3 Read aloud the paragraph in "The Heat Is On!" that tells what the "greenhouse effect" is. Talk about this with a partner.

4 What does the caption on page 61 describe? Read this caption aloud to a partner.

> A caption is an explanation of a photograph.

Digital Learning

For a list of links and activities that relate to this Science standard, visit the California Treasures Web site at www.macmillanmh.com to access the Content Reader resources.

Have students view the e-Review "Changes Affect Living Things." In addition, distribute copies of the Translated Concept Summaries in Spanish, Chinese, Hmong, Khmer, and Vietnamese.

Changes Affect Animals

Animals have body parts and ways of acting that help them survive where they live. Zebras have flat teeth for chewing grass. Fish have gills for getting oxygen from water.

What would happen to an animal if its **habitat**, or home, changed? For example, what would happen if there was no rain in an area. Water could dry up. Grasses could die. Animals would not have food or water.

Some animals find a way to survive by changing how they live. If the changes last a long time, some animals move to a new habitat.

◄ Animals such as this springbok depend on watering holes.

There may be no rain for a long time in the savanna. Grasses can dry up. Watering holes can dry up too. Zebras and other animals move to new habitats to find food and water. Fish in a pond cannot move to a new home. If their habitat goes dry, they may die.

▲ Animals migrate, or move to another place, in search of food and water if their habitat changes.

◀ Many frogs are able to burrow and survive underground when a pond dries up.

TROUBLE in the Ocean

What's causing "dead zones" in oceans around the world?

The world's oceans are filled with life. However, over the past 40 years, dead zones have appeared in almost 150 places around the globe.

Dead zones are areas where no animals live. The water below the surface in these areas has no oxygen in it. Without oxygen, fish and other sea creatures die.

The light colors show the dead zone.

Too Much of a Good Thing

We know what causes dead zones—fertilizers used on farms and lawns. Fertilizers help plants to grow. In the ocean, fertilizers are deadly.

When it rains, the water carries fertilizers from land into rivers. The rivers flow into the ocean and the fertilizers are dumped in one place.

Now the fertilizers help tiny plantlike algae to grow on the ocean. When the algae die, they sink to the bottom. There bacteria eat them. The bacteria use up all the oxygen in the water. Then nothing can live there. It is a dead zone.

Saving the Ocean

How do we stop dead zones? One solution is to plant trees and grass next to rivers to soak up fertilizers. Another solution is to use less of the fertilizers.

▲ Green algae on the ocean surface

Cause/Effect Writing Frame

**Use the Writing Frame below to orally summarize
"Changes Affect Animals."**

When a habitat changes, the animals that are able to live there can be harmed.

If the changes last a long time, **then** _____ .

For example, if there is no rain, it can **affect** animals. No rain for

a long time can **cause** _____

_____ .

No rain can also **cause** _____

_____ .

If a habitat for fish stays dry for too long, **then** _____

_____ .

Therefore, one main **effect** of change is _____

_____ .

Use the frame to write the summary on another sheet of paper.
Be sure to include the **bold** signal words. Keep this as a model
of this Text Structure.

Critical Thinking

1 Another name for a home is a _____ .

   A. mud

   B. harm

   C. habitat

2 Find the sentence in "Trouble in the Ocean" that tells why an area is called a dead zone.

3 Point to the sentences in the same article that tell about one solution to dead zones.

4 Discuss with a partner the photograph of the elephants on page 67. Describe what they are doing.

A photograph is a picture taken with a camera.

Digital Learning

For a list of links and activities that relate to this Science standard, visit the California Treasures Web site at www.macmillanmh.com to access the Content Reader resources.

Have students view the e-Review "Changes Affect Living Things." In addition, distribute copies of the Translated Concept Summaries in Spanish, Chinese, Hmong, Khmer, and Vietnamese.

Sudden Changes in the Environment

Mammoths once lived in North America. They looked something like elephants of Africa and Asia today. Then something happened. The mammoths disappeared.

Ten thousand years ago, North America was in an ice age. Sheets of ice covered much of the United States. Large animals, such as mammoths and saber-toothed cats, lived in this cold environment. Then the climate changed. Temperatures got hotter. The ice started to melt. The plants that mammoths ate disappeared. Finally, the mammoths became extinct. **Extinct** means that there are no more of a type of living thing alive.

◀ Scientists think hunting is one reason woolly mammoths disappeared. Climate change is another reason.

Living Things Respond to Change

Change	Living Thing	What May Happen	Why
warmer climate	saber-toothed cat	becomes extinct	cannot find food; cannot survive in warm climate
volcanic eruption	short-tailed albatross	survives	can fly to new environment
colder climate	bear	survives	can grow thicker fur

Climate change may cause kinds of plants or animals to become extinct. Disease and human activities may also cause them to become extinct.

When a new kind of animal, for example, moves into an ecosystem, the other living things can be in danger. Some plants and animals may die. Others can survive sudden changes. Some can move to new places. The survivors will continue to reproduce.

One Enormous Crocodile!

A fossil found in Africa tells of a giant crocodile that lived 110 million years ago.

Paul Sereno and the super croc's skull.

Paul Sereno is a dinosaur hunter. In 2000, he was in the country of Niger, in Africa. One day he dug up the bones of an enormous crocodile, or super croc. It lived 105 million years before humans existed. When it was alive, it had plenty of dinosaurs to eat. Then, 110 million years ago, it became extinct.

◀ super croc found here

Super Croc Was Big

The super croc was 40 feet long—as long as a school bus! It weighed as much as a small whale. Its jaws were five feet long. The crocodile that Sereno found was not even full size.

The super croc is a kind of animal called *flesh crocodile emperor*. That is a good name for this huge meat-eater.

▼ super croc's teeth

A Fighter

The super croc lived and hunted in the African rivers. It was a great fighter. Its body, head, and part of its tail were covered in hard, bony plates. These bony plates protected the croc from attacks. Also, there were more than 100 teeth in its long, narrow jaw. It could easily kill a dinosaur.

The super croc could lie underwater. It waited for an animal to come near the shore. Then it dragged the animal into the water to kill it. —*Bill Doyle*

All Sizes

Alligators and crocodiles belong to the same group of reptiles. These animals today are much smaller than the super croc.

Name: Sarcosuchus imperator (super croc)
Habitat: The rivers of central Africa
Weight: About 17,500 pounds
Length: Up to 50 feet long

Portia Sloan/National Geographic Society

E.R. Degginger/Bruce Coleman

Name: Australian crocodile
Habitat: Saltwater and freshwater areas in northern Australia and Asia
Weight: About 2,000 pounds
Length: Up to 23 feet

Name: American alligator
Habitat: Freshwater swamps and lakes in southeastern U.S.
Weight: 1,300 pounds
Length: Up to 20 feet

M.H. Sharp/Photo Researchers

Problem/Solution Writing Frame

**Use the Writing Frame to orally summarize
"Sudden Changes in the Environment."**

Ten thousand years ago, North America was in an ice age.
Mammoths lived there.

After the ice age, mammoths had a **problem** because

the ice _____ .

This led to another **problem** for mammoths. The plants _____

_____ .

The mammoths started to die, and in time they _____

_____ .

When a new kind of living thing moves into an ecosystem, other

living things _____

_____ .

Some living things can survive sudden changes, but _____

_____ .

Use the Writing Frame to write the summary on another sheet
of paper. Be sure to include the **bold** signal words. Keep this as
a model of this Text Structure.

Critical Thinking

1 If there are no more of a type of living thing alive, then that thing is _____.

    A. disappearing

    B. extinct

    C. environment

2 Show a partner where in "One Enormous Crocodile!" a super croc is first described.

3 Read aloud the text in this article that gives information about a super croc's length and weight.

4 Describe the chart on page 73 to a partner.

A chart is a drawing that shows information in the form of a table, graph, or picture.

Digital Learning

For links and activities that relate to this Science standard, visit the California Treasures Web site at www.macmillanmh.com to access the Content Reader resources.

Have students view the Science e-Review "Living Things of the Past." In addition, distribute copies of the Translated Concept Summaries in Spanish, Chinese, Hmong, Khmer, and Vietnamese.

We Study the Night Sky

A star is a hot, glowing ball of gases. The Sun is a medium-size star. We see other stars as tiny points of light in the night sky. They seem tiny because they are very far away.

Look at the night sky on a clear evening. Choose a group of stars, or **constellation**. You can make a drawing to remember what they look like and where they are.

After one hour, the stars are not in the same place. The stars did not move. They only appeared to move because the Earth rotates on its axis.

As Earth revolves around the Sun, we see different stars. In winter, you cannot see the stars that were in the summer sky. These stars are now on the opposite side of our orbit. In summer, you have moved to the other side of the Sun. So in summer you cannot see constellations you saw in winter.

▼ Can you see the constellation Orion in summer or winter?

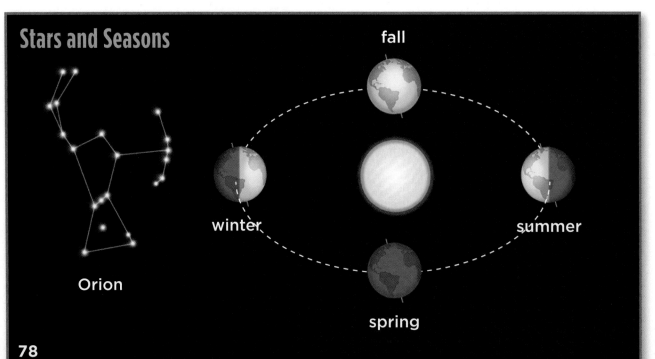

Stars and Seasons

fall

winter

summer

spring

Orion

light from stars

path of light

eyepiece

lens

The stars, the planets, and the Moon are very far away. Scientists use telescopes to study objects in space. A **telescope** is a tool that gathers light to make faraway objects appear larger, closer, and clearer. We can see many more planets and stars through a telescope than by unaided eyes.

Space is one of the best places for a telescope. The Hubble Space Telescope travels around Earth. It takes pictures and sends them back to Earth.

Scientists study space with other kinds of telescopes. Radio telescopes collect radio waves. We cannot see radio waves. Scientists use computers to change radio waves into pictures.

radio telescope

The Hubble Space Telescope

The Hubble Space Telescope has helped scientists see deep into the universe.

It cost $2 billion to put the Hubble Space Telescope into orbit around Earth. It was a lot of hard work. Then, in 1990, astronomers found a problem. The telescope's mirror was imperfect. Astronauts had to fix it. They flew to the telescope on the Space Shuttle. It was dangerous. The astronauts put a new mirror in the telescope.

Gases in Earth's atmosphere make it hard for people on the ground to see space. Even the best telescopes on Earth cannot see clearly. The Hubble is outside Earth's atmosphere. This helps it get a clear view of space.

▲ An astronaut fixes the Hubble's mirror.

Hubble Discovers Many Things

Hubble Helps

The Hubble uses its cameras to take pictures. The Hubble also has equipment to see objects invisible to humans.

The Hubble has taken 500,000 pictures of more than 25,000 objects in space. It has made 100,000 trips around Earth. This important telescope collects a lot of information every day. Then it sends the information to scientists on Earth.

The Future of Hubble

Scientists do not know exactly how much longer the Hubble will work. They work hard to keep the Hubble looking into space. —*Lisa Jo Rudy*

* The Hubble saw two new moons orbiting Pluto.

* The Hubble found more than 15 Jupiter-size planets in the middle of our galaxy, the Milky Way.

* The Hubble took pictures that helped scientists learn more about exploding stars.

* The Hubble helped scientists learn that the universe is about 13.7 billion years old.

▼ Hubble took this photograph. It shows the birth of stars.

Royalty-Free/CORBIS

Compare/Contrast Writing Frame

**Use the Writing Frame to orally summarize
"We Study the Night Sky."**

Stars have **many interesting features**. Stars are all **alike**

in that they are all _____

_____ .

The Sun is a medium-sized star. **However**, we see other far

away stars as _____ .

Telescopes have **many interesting features**. Telescopes are

alike in that they make faraway objects _____

_____ .

The Hubble Space Telescope is **unlike** most telescopes because

it _____

_____ .

Radio telescopes are **different from** the Hubble telescope

because radio telescopes _____

_____ .

Use the Writing Frame to write the summary on another sheet
of paper. Keep it as a model of this Text Structure.

Critical Thinking

1 A group of stars is called a _____.

    A. telescope

    B. planet

    C. constellation

2 Point out the sentence in "The Hubble Space Telescope" that explains the problem astronomers found. Discuss the solution with a partner.

3 With a partner, read aloud the parts of the text from "The Hubble Space Telescope" that tell what Hubble can do.

4 Describe for a partner what the diagram on page 78 shows.

A diagram is a plan. It explains the way something works.

Digital Learning

For a list of links and activities that relate to this Science standard, visit the California Treasures Web site at www.macmillanmh.com to access the Content Reader resources.

Have students view the e-Review "What Is a Telescope?"

In addition, distribute copies of the Translated Concept Summaries in Spanish, Chinese, Hmong, Khmer, and Vietnamese.

Science

The Moon's Shape

The Moon is shaped like a ball. The Moon's shape always stays the same. So why does the Moon look different from night to night?

The Moon moves through space. The Moon orbits Earth. Earth orbits the Sun. The Moon's shape seems to change because of its orbit. Look at the diagram. One half of the Moon faces the Sun. The Sun lights this part. The other half faces away from the Sun. This part is in darkness. The Moon does not make light. The Moon orbits Earth and we see different parts of it lighted. We see these lighted parts as different shapes, or phases.

The Moon orbits Earth in about four weeks. It passes through all of its phases during this time. The four-week cycle of changing phases is called the **lunar cycle**.

Moon's Orbit

sunlight

new Moon
You cannot see a new Moon.

sun

third quarter Moon
Our view of the
Moon from Earth
21 days after the
new Moon

full Moon
Our view of the
Moon from Earth
14 days after the
new Moon

first quarter Moon
Our view of the Moon
from Earth 7 days
after the new Moon

Is Pluto a Planet?

Jerry LoFaro

▲ Pluto and two
of its moons

**Astronomers
decide Pluto
cannot be
called a planet.**

Pluto was discovered in 1930.
Scientists named it the ninth planet in
our solar system. Some scientists disagreed.
They did not think Pluto was really a planet.
One reason is that it is smaller than the
planets. It has an unusual tilt and travels in an
odd orbit. In 2006, scientists met in Prague,
Czech Republic. The International
Astronomical Union decided that
Pluto is not a planet!

Pluto has always been different. It
is very small and very far away from
the Sun. This makes it very cold and
very dark. This is why it was not
discovered until 1930. When
Charles Tombaugh discovered it,
he named it after the Roman god
of the underworld.

This is Pluto with Charon. Two
smaller moons are next to it. ▼

NASA, ESA, H. Weaver (JHU/APL),
A. Stern (SwRI) and the HST Pluto
Companion Search Team

Dan Durda/NASA-JPL

In 1975, astronomers saw a tiny moon around Pluto. They named it Charon. In 2005, two more moons were discovered.

Finally, astronomers decided that only Mercury, Venus, Earth, Mars, Jupiter, Saturn, Uranus, and Neptune are classical planets. This means that they are big and almost round, like a ball. Each of the classical planets has its own orbit. Pluto's orbit is part of Neptune's path. Pluto is now classified as a dwarf planet.

▲ This drawing shows the New Horizon spacecraft coming near Pluto. Charon is in the background.

In January 2006, NASA launched the *New Horizons* spacecraft to study Pluto and beyond Pluto.

Richard Blinzel, a professor at Massachusetts Institute of Technology agrees: "Many more Plutos wait to be discovered."

Pluto vs. Earth

Is Pluto different from Earth? Look at the chart.

	Pluto	Earth
surface	mostly covered by frozen nitrogen and rock	mostly covered by water (70%) and land
diameter	about 1,400 miles	about 8,000 miles
number of Moons	3	1
average distance from the Sun	3.5 billion miles	93 million miles
orbit	It takes 248 Earth years to travel around the Sun.	It takes 365 days to travel around the Sun.
length of one day	about 154 hours	24 hours

Description Writing Frame

Use the Writing Frame to orally summarize "The Moon's Shape."

There is much **interesting information** about the Moon.

For example, the Moon is shaped _____

_____.

The Moon's shape always _____

_____.

The Moon **moves** _____

_____.

The Moon orbits _____.

The Moon's shape seems to change because _____

_____.

In the lunar cycle, we see all of the Moon's phases. **For example**,

we see the _____

_____.

Use the Writing Frame to write the summary on another sheet of paper. Be sure to include the **bold** signal words. Keep this as a model of this Text Structure.

Critical Thinking

1 The four-week cycle of changing phases is called
   the _____.

   A. lunar cycle

   B. Moon walk

   C. lighted half

2 Show a partner the sentences in "Is Pluto a Planet?" that give
   facts about Pluto.

3 Find the chart in "Is Pluto a Planet?" How are Pluto and Earth
   different?

4 Discuss the diagram on pages 84 and 85 with
   a partner. Talk about why the Moon appears to
   change shape.

A diagram is a
plan. It explains the
way something works.

Digital Learning

For a list of links and activities that relate to this Science standard,
visit the California Treasures Web site at www.macmillanmh.com to
access the Content Reader resources.

Have students view the Science in this article e-Review "The Moon."
In addition, distribute copies of the Translated Concept Summaries
in Spanish, Chinese, Hmong, Khmer, and Vietnamese.

Science

Earth and the Sun

The Sun seems to move across the sky in an arc each day. In the morning, the Sun appears on the eastern horizon. A **horizon** is an imaginary line where the land seems to meet the sky. The Sun appears high in the sky at midday. The Sun appears close to the western horizon in the evening.

The Sun appears to move across the sky. Actually it stays in one place. It is Earth that is spinning. As Earth spins, places on Earth move past the Sun.

At any moment, one side of Earth faces the Sun and has daytime. The side facing away from the Sun has nighttime. As Earth spins, places on Earth go from day to night and back to day over and over.

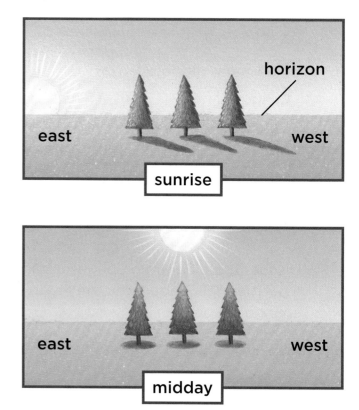

east   horizon   west
sunrise

east   west
midday

east   west
sunset

90

Seasons change as Earth rotates on its axis and revolves in a regular path around the Sun. An object that moves around another object **revolves**. Seasons change because Earth is tilted on its axis. This axis is always tilted in the same direction during Earth's orbit.

The Sun's position in the sky also seems to change from season to season. The Sun is high up at noon when it is summer in California. At that time of the year, the northern half of Earth is tilted toward the Sun. This tilt makes the Sun's path seem higher in the sky.

The path of the Sun appears low at noon when it is winter in California. The southern half of Earth is tilted toward the Sun. California is tilted away from the Sun.

Earth Revolves Around the Sun

spring

winter

summer

fall

SOLAR ECLIPSE!

A solar eclipse leaves some people on Earth in the shadow of the moon.

A total solar eclipse happens when the orbits of the Sun, the Moon, and Earth line up exactly. The Moon passes directly between Earth and the Sun. This blocks the sunlight. The shadow of the Moon falls across Earth. It looks like night. Then, the Sun comes back!

Where Did the Sun Go?

A total solar eclipse is possible because of a coincidence. The Moon and the Sun look about the same size in the sky. The Sun is really much bigger than the Moon.

The Moon blocks the Sun's light in a total solar eclipse. ▶

The Sun is 400 times bigger than the Moon. The Sun is 400 times farther away than the Moon, too. This is why the two objects appear to be the same size. So, when the Moon and Sun line up, the Moon is big enough to block out the Sun.

The Moon appears as a black circle over the Sun during a solar eclipse. The Moon moves slowly across the Sun until it blocks it completely. Then the Sun begins to appear on the other side. A solar eclipse lasts for about three hours. The time of total darkness is only a few minutes. —*Andrea Delbanco*

See Eclipses Safely

You can hurt your eyes if you looked at the Sun. Be safe if you view a solar eclipse. Here are some ways to stay safe.

✹ Never look directly at the Sun with just your eyes or with a telescope or binoculars.

✹ You can make a pinhole camera to see solar eclipses safely. First, make a small hole in a piece of cardboard. Tilt the cardboard until the Sun shines through the hole. Put a piece of white paper behind the hole. Make sure the Sun hits it. Then look at the white paper. You will see a safe, clear picture of the solar eclipse.

The Moon can block the Sun's light. ▼

Sun

Moon

Umbra

Earth

Penumbra

Kevin Hailey

Compare/Contrast Writing Frame

Use the Writing Frame to orally summarize "Earth and the Sun."

The Sun and Earth are **both** in the _____ .

The Sun seems to move across the sky because Earth _____

_____ .

When one side of Earth faces the Sun, this side of Earth

_____ .

In contrast, the side that faces away from the Sun _____ .

The Sun's position in the sky seems to change from season to

season. **However**, Earth's axis is always _____ .

When it is summer in California, the Sun _____ .

However, the Sun's path seems lower in California during _____

_____ .

One way the Sun and Earth are **different** is that Earth revolves in _____

_____ .

Use the Writing Frame to write the summary on another sheet
of paper. Be sure to include the **bold** signal word. Keep it as a
model of this Text Structure.

Critical Thinking

1 An object that moves around another object
   _____.

   A. revolves

   B. tilts

   C. returns

2 Point out the sentence in "Solar Eclipse!" that tells what a total solar eclipse is. Discuss a solar eclipse with a partner.

3 Show a partner where the text in "Solar Eclipse!" tells how to see solar eclipses safely.

4 With a partner, contrast the diagrams on pages 90 and 91.

A diagram is a plan. It explains the way something works.

Digital Learning

For a list of links and activities that relate to this Science standard, visit the California Treasures Web site at www.macmillanmh.com to access the Content Reader resources.

Have students view the Science in Motion video "Earth Revolves Around the Sun."

In addition, distribute copies of the Translated Concept Summaries in Spanish, Chinese, Hmong, Khmer, and Vietnamese.

Science

DIFFERENT KINDS OF LAND

California has many kinds of land and water. Our state has mountains with snowy tops. It has hot, dry deserts. It has low, flat land. California has lakes and long rivers too.

▲ Some parts of California are deserts.

Two kinds of landforms in California are hills and mountains. Landforms are the shapes on Earth's surface. California also has plains. Plains are large areas of flat land.

California has valleys, too. A valley is low land between hills or mountains. Valleys often have rivers. The large Central Valley runs down the middle of California.

California has lakes, rivers, and streams. It is next to an ocean. These are called bodies of water. Salt water is in oceans. Fresh water is in lakes, rivers, ponds and streams.

California has many miles of coastline.

Geography is the land and water of a place. It also includes the way people, plants, and animals live on and in land and water. Geographers, or people who study geography, divide California into eight regions. A region is an area with common features that make it different from other areas. Kinds of landforms, bodies of water, and climate all shape a region. Climate is the kind of weather a place has. For example, the Sierra Nevada region is famous for its snowy mountains.

Landforms, climate, and bodies of water affect how people live. They are different from region to region. So the way people live varies from region to region. Look at the map. Think about where you live. Is your area flat or hilly? Is it near the ocean? Is it in a valley? What landforms are in your region?

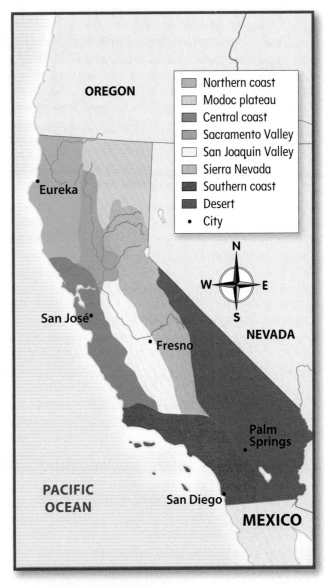

▲ Each region of California is a different color on the map.

California Ecosystems

More people come to California. Then they build more houses.

JupiterImage/Thinkstock/Alamy

California is enormous. It covers 160,000 square miles. It has deserts and mountains. It has seacoasts and valleys, too. 30,000 insects, 563 kinds of birds, and about 8,000 plants live in our state's ecosystems. That is more than any other state.

Animals live in the ecosystem that is best for them. Jackrabbits live in the desert. Seals live in the ocean. Elk and deer live in the grasslands. People must protect these ecosystems to protect the animals of California.

Almost 40 million people live in California. More people are coming. They build more houses and roads. Then some animals will have no place to live. The state of California is passing laws to protect the land.

The California Deserts

California has many deserts. Deserts are dry and often hot. They have amazing plants and animals. Saguaro cactus, bighorn sheep, sidewinder snakes, desert tortoises, jackrabbits, and roadrunners live in California deserts.

Joshua Tree National Park

Robert Marien/Corbis

These deserts are in valleys and in highlands. The Mojave National Preserve, Death Valley, and Joshua Tree National Park are some of the most famous California deserts.

Deserts form in different ways in California. Volcanoes and earthquakes formed some deserts. Other deserts were once ancient seas.

Redwood Forests

Northern California has some of the tallest, oldest trees in the world. California redwoods can live for more than 2,000 years. They can grow over 369 feet tall. They live in wet and cool places—in forests near the Pacific Ocean. Fog comes in summer. Storms hit in winter.

The animals in these forests can live in the cool, wet weather. Some animals that live there are bears, pine martens, and many types of birds. There are also giant salamanders, red-bellied newts, silver salmon, and steelhead trout.

The California redwoods are in danger. Logging and pollution are threats. The law protects some parts of these forests. —Lisa Jo Rudy

Redwood Forest

Redwood Forest

Death Valley

Mojave National Preserve

Joshua Tree National Park

Key

Redwood Forest

Desert

Map Resources/Punchstock

California redwoods

Creatas/Punchstock

Description Writing Frame

**Use the Writing Frame to orally summarize
"Different Kinds of Land."**

California has **many interesting** kinds of land and water.

For example, California has _____

_____ .

Earth has shapes on its surface. **For example**, California has

hills and _____ .

California **also** has _____ ,

which are large areas of _____ .

California has valleys, **too**. A valley is _____

_____ .

California has bodies of water. You can find salt water in _____

_____ .

Bodies of fresh water are _____ .

Use the Writing Frame to write the summary on another sheet
of paper. Be sure to include **bold** signal words. Keep this as a
model of this Text Structure.

Critical Thinking

1. The land and water of a place and the way people, plants, and animals live on them is called _____.

   A. climate

   B. landforms

   C. geography

2. Point out the sentences in "California Ecosystems" that describe California's deserts.

3. Show a partner the sentences in "California Ecosystems" that tell about California redwoods.

4. Use the map on page 97 to discuss the different regions of California with a partner.

A map is a drawing that shows where different places are.

Digital Learning

For a list of links and activities that relate to this History/Social Science standard, visit the California Treasures Web site at www.macmillanmh.com to access the Content Reader resources. Have students view the video "Communities and Geography." In addition, distribute copies of the Translated Concept Summaries in Spanish, Chinese, Hmong, Khmer, and Vietnamese.

PEOPLE CHANGE LAND AND WATER

People can change how they live so they can live in their environment. They also change the environment to meet their needs. People change the environment when they build **dams.** A dam is a wall across a river or stream that holds back and controls the water. Dams let people store water. Then, people use the water when they need it. People built a dam across the Sacramento River in Northern California. The water formed Shasta Lake. Now people can send water from Shasta Lake to the Sacramento Valley in the south.

This is a dam in California. ▼

Los Angeles was once a small town that got its water from the Los Angeles River. The town needed more water as it grew into a city. So, people bought the rights to the land and water of the Owens River Valley. They built an **aqueduct** to bring water from the Owens River to Los Angeles. An aqueduct is a long, human-made pipe. It is used to move water from one place to another.

The Los Angeles Aqueduct was built through mountains and across deserts. The workers dug tunnels through the mountains.

They also made new roads, and built railroad tracks to carry supplies. They built power lines and telephone lines. All these things changed the environment.

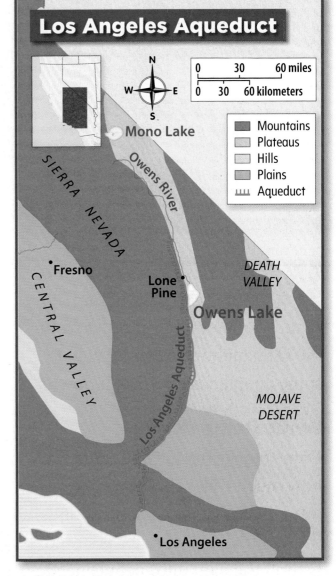

Los Angeles Aqueduct

Mono Lake

Owens River

SIERRA NEVADA

Fresno

Lone Pine

DEATH VALLEY

Owens Lake

CENTRAL VALLEY

Los Angeles Aqueduct

MOJAVE DESERT

Los Angeles

	0	30	60 miles
	0	30	60 kilometers

Mountains
Plateaus
Hills
Plains
Aqueduct

▲ The Los Angeles Aqueduct goes from the Owens River to Los Angeles.

It took five years to build the Los Angeles Aqueduct. ▶

103

People Decide the Future of a Dam

Where does your water come from? People in the San Francisco Bay Area get water from the O'Shaughnessy Dam. Why do some people want to take it down?

What Dams Do

Dams block rivers. They control how much water can flow. The water behind a dam rises. It floods the land there. The water is stored behind the dam until people need it. Dams control water that is used to produce electricity. Water from dams can also be used to drink or to irrigate crops.

The Lost Valley

The O'Shaughnessy Dam is located in the western part of Yosemite National Park. People built the dam in 1913 on the Tuolumne River.

Water behind the dam flooded the Hetch Hetchy Valley. This valley was beautiful. It had large waterfalls and cliffs. Now the natural wonders of the valley are underwater.

MOUNT HOLYOKE COLLEGE ART MUSEUM

This painting shows the Hetch Hetchy Valley before it was flooded.

People Debate the Dam

A group called Restore Hetch Hetchy wants to take down the O'Shaughnessy Dam. Then the Tuolumne can flow freely again. People will see the beautiful valley.

Other people want to keep the dam. It provides water and electricity to 2.4 million people and thousands of businesses. The cost to find other sources of water and electricity are too high.

Dams:
Solutions and Problems

Dams were solutions to important problems. They provided water and electricity. Now people ask: "Why can't rivers run free so we can uncover the land?"

Barrie Rokeach

▲ **The O'Shaughnessy Dam holds back the Tuolumne River.**

However, if we take away dams, where will water and electricity come from?

People will debate dams for a long time. What will the answer be for the O'Shaughnessy Dam? —*Susan Moger*

Ei Katsumata/Alamy

The O'Shaughnessy Dam

Problem/Solution Writing Frame

**Use the Writing Frame to orally summarize
"People Change Land and Water."**

People change the environment to meet their needs. When

people need to **solve** a water **problem**, they may _____

_____ .

Los Angeles was once a small town. It had a **problem** when

_____

_____ .

People **solved** this **problem** when they _____

_____ .

Then there was a new **problem**. The Los Angeles Aqueduct

was built _____

_____ .

So, the workers had to do things that _____

_____ .

Use the Writing Frame to write the summary on another sheet
of paper. Be sure to include the **bold** signal words. Keep this as
a model of this Text Structure.

Critical Thinking

1 A long, human-made pipe that is used to move water is called a(n) _____.

   A. railroad

   B. aqueduct

   C. aquarium

2 Point out the sentences in "People Decide the Future of a Dam" that explain what dams do.

3 With a partner, read aloud the text in "People Decide the Future of a Dam" that tells where the O'Shaughnessy Dam is located.

4 Use your finger to trace the Los Angeles Aqueduct on the map on page 103.

> A map is a drawing that shows where different places are.

Digital Learning

For a list of links and activities that relate to this History/Social Science standard, visit the California Treasures Web site at www.macmillanmh.com to access the Content Reader resources. Have students explore "Your Community's Land and Resources." In addition, distribute copies of the Translated Concept Summaries in Spanish, Chinese, Hmong, Khmer, and Vietnamese.

THE FIRST CALIFORNIANS

Native Americans were the first people to live in what is now California. They lived in different groups. Each had its own **culture**. Culture is the way of life a group of people shares. Culture includes language, food, arts, and beliefs.

The Miwok Native Americans lived in the Central Valley. Oak trees there provided acorns. The nuts were part of their culture.

The Miwok had songs about acorns and used them to make bread. Each year the Miwok held a festival to celebrate the importance of acorns. Miwok people still hold this festival today.

The Chumash Native Americans lived in large villages along the southern coast. They got much of their food from the ocean. They built large canoes for fishing.

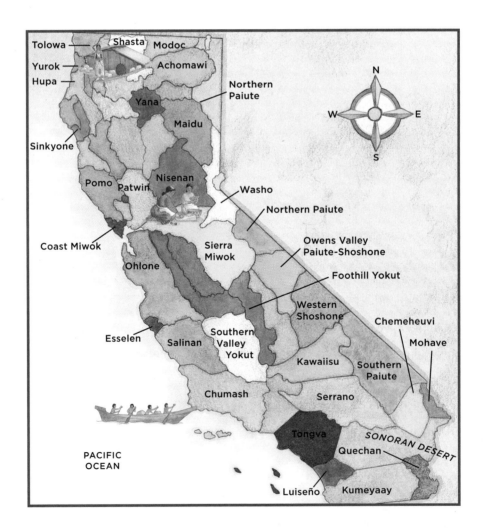

The Kawaiisu Native Americans moved from place to place as the seasons changed. In the winter they lived in sunny valleys of the Mojave Desert. They built waterproof shelters of branches and bark. They warmed their homes with heated rocks. In the summer they moved up into the cool Tehachapi Mountains. Girls and women gathered berries, nuts, and acorns to eat. Boys and men hunted deer. The Kawaiisu also painted designs on rocks and rock walls. They made **petroglyphs**, or rock carvings.

▲ This headdress was made by the Hupa people. It was used on special occasions.

The Hupa Native Americans lived in villages along the Trinity River. They gathered berries and nuts to eat. They hunted deer and elk. They made nets to catch fish in the river. The Hupa built strong houses from cedarwood.

Hupa dancers in the Jump Dance ▶

AMERICANS CELEBRATE AMERICAN INDIAN HERITAGE

A powwow in Indio, California

Americans celebrate National American Indian and Alaska Native Heritage Month during November. We think about the culture and history of American Indians (also known as Native Americans) and Alaska Natives at this time.

We Honor Heritage

The celebration of American Indian heritage started in 1916. At that time, Americans observed American Indian Day each year in May. In 1990, President George H. W. Bush declared November as National American Indian Heritage Month.

In 2004 the federal government opened the National Museum of the American Indian in Washington, D.C. This Smithsonian museum honors the history, arts, and lives of Native Americans.

AP Photo/Lawrence Jackson

The National Museum of the American Indian opened in 2004. This Eskimo mask is on display there.

The Granger Collection, NY

American Indian and Alaska Native History

Native Americans and Alaska Natives lived in what is now North and South America. They lived there for thousands of years before explorers arrived in the 1400s. Then Christopher Columbus reached the islands off southeastern North America in 1492. He called the people he met Indians. He thought he had sailed to India.

There were between 12 million and 15 million American Indians and Alaska Natives before Europeans arrived. Disease and war killed hundreds of thousands of American Indians after Europeans colonized the land.

Today, there are 4.1 million American Indians and Alaska Natives in the U.S. More than 100 American Indian tribes live in California. That is about 440,000 Native American people. —*Jill Egan*

Frank and Frances Carpenter collection/ Library of Congress

▲ An Eskimo man and his child

Did you know?

There are more than 550 American Indian groups in the United States.

The largest Alaska Native group is the Tlingit. It has about 17,200 people.

538,000 American Indians and Alaska Natives live on reservations.

Cause/Effect Writing Frame

Use the Writing Frame to orally summarize "The First Californians."

Native Americans were the first people to live in what is now California. **Because** the Miwok Native Americans lived in the

Central Valley with oak trees, _____

_____ .

As a result, _____

_____ .

The **effect** of this today is that the Miwok people still _____

_____ .

Because they wanted to keep warm in the winter, the Kawaiisu

lived in _____ .

Because they wanted to keep cool in the summer, they moved

up into _____ .

For the Hupa Native Americans, the **effect** of living along a river

was that they learned to make _____ .

Use the Writing Frame to write the summary on another sheet of paper. Be sure to include **bold** signal words. Keep this as a model of this Text Structure.

Critical Thinking

1 A way of life that a people share is called a _____.

   A. culture

   B. Chumash

   C. petroglyph

2 Find the sentence in "Americans Celebrate American Indian Heritage" that tells what Americans celebrate during the month of November.

3 Revisit "Americans Celebrate American Indian Heritage" to reread why Christopher Columbus called the people he met Indians.

4 Talk about the different California Native American groups with a partner. Use the map on page 108 to discuss where they lived.

A map is a drawing that shows where different places are.

Digital Learning

For a list of links and activities that relate to this History/Social Science standard, visit the California Treasures Web site at www.macmillanmh.com to access the Content Reader resources. Have students view the video "Native American Communities." In addition, distribute copies of the Translated Concept Summaries in Spanish, Chinese, Hmong, Khmer, and Vietnamese.

LIFE IN A KUMEYAAY VILLAGE

The Kumeyaay have lived in Southern California for thousands of years. The warm climate of this area made it an ideal place to live. The environment provided food, water, shelter, and medicine.

Animals provided food. Their skins provided clothes, rugs, and blankets. The Kumeyaay hunted animals with bows and arrows made from willow branches and deer **ligaments**. Ligaments are strong bands of stretchy tissue that connect bones. Hunters used arrows with stone arrowheads for large animals, such as deer and bighorn sheep. Women used **snares**, or traps, to catch small animals such as rabbits. Sometimes small animals were hunted with wooden arrowheads.

▲ The Kumeyaay made bows from willow branches.

◄ The Kumeyaay used the agave plant to treat cuts and infections.

The Kumeyaay moved during the year. They hunted and gathered food. In the winter, many lived on the coast. They fished and gathered clams. Their winter houses were huts made of willow branches with leaves. Each house had a small door. It was covered with a mat or basket at night. This kept out the cold air.

The Kumeyaay moved into the mountains for the summer. They collected wild plums and other fruits. Summer shelters were simple, such as caves.

The Kumeyaay gathered nuts and acorns in the fall. They collected many nuts and acorns to eat in the winter.

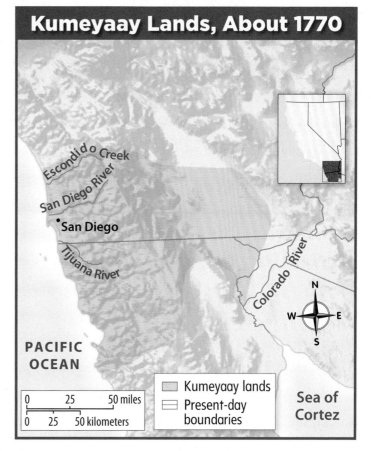

Kumeyaay Lands, About 1770

Escondido Creek
San Diego River
San Diego
Tijuana River
Colorado River
PACIFIC OCEAN
Sea of Cortez

N W E S

0 25 50 miles	
0 25 50 kilometers	

☐ Kumeyaay lands
▤ Present-day boundaries

The Kumeyaay used baskets like this to collect acorns. ▶

MANY TRIBES, MANY CULTURES

Native American groups in California had different ways of life depending on where they lived.

Many groups of Native Americans have lived in California for thousands of years. Some tribes lived in the forests, near lakes and rivers. They built villages, hunted, and fished.

Other tribes lived near the sea. They built strong canoes, fished in the sea, and hunted for seafood.

Desert tribes searched for food and water. They became skilled hunters and gatherers. They traveled to a new place when food became scarce.

The Chumash People of the Sea

The Chumash people lived in what is now Southern California. They lived in villages along the Pacific Coast.

Butler Institute of American Art/The Bridgeman Art Library

▲ **A Native American camp in what is now Yosemite National Park**

▶ A reconstructed Chumash house

They got their food from the sea. Their wooden canoes could be 30 feet long. They could hold 12 people.

Most Chumash lived in houses of woven bulrushes and cattails. Some lived in houses made of whale bones. The Chumash used shells for money. They wore few clothes when it was warm. They wore animal skins when it was cold.

Today the Chumash tribe is still active. Many Californians are all or part Chumash.

The Serrano People of Central California

The Serrano people lived in Big Bear Valley in Central California. They lived near springs, streams, and rivers. They ate nuts, berries, herbs, and roots. They hunted small animals. They wore clothing made of deerskin. Serrano women made beautiful pottery.

Serrano woman, 1924

Serrano people built small villages. They dug circles and built frames of poles to build their homes. The poles were covered with brush. —*Lisa Jo Rudy*

Serrano man, 1924

◀ **Chumash basket**

Description Writing Frame

Use the Writing Frame to orally summarize "Life in a Kumeyaay Village."

The Kumeyaay lived in Southern California because the

environment provided _____

_____.

The Kumeyaay hunted with tools made from the environment.

For example, bows and arrows were made from _____

_____.

Arrowheads were made from _____

_____.

The animals of Southern California were **important** to the Kumeyaay

because _____.

In the winter the Kumeyaay lived on the coast. This

environment provided food **such as** _____.

Use the Writing Frame to write the summary on another sheet of paper. Be sure to include the **bold** signal words. Keep this as a model of this Text Structure.

Critical Thinking

1 Strong bands of stretchy tissue that connect bones are called _____.

   A. ligaments

   B. leaves

   C. blankets

2 Point to the sentence in "Many Tribes, Many Cultures" that tells where the Chumash people lived.

3 With a partner, read aloud the text from "Many Tribes, Many Cultures" that tells what Serrano women made.

4 Use the map on page 115 to tell a partner about the Kumeyaay lands in California.

> A map is a drawing that shows where different places are.

Digital Learning

For a list of links and activities that relate to this History/Social Science standard, visit the California Treasures Web site at www.macmillanmh.com to access the Content Reader resources. Have students visit "A Native American Child in California." In addition, distribute copies of the Translated Concept Summaries in Spanish, Chinese, Hmong, Khmer, and Vietnamese.

LEADERSHIP OF THE KUMEYAAY

The Kumeyaay people lived in groups, or bands. Each band had its own land and resources. The Kumeyaay had many people and covered a large area. So, they set up a **government**. A government is a group of people who lead a community, state, or nation.

Much of the Kumeyaay land was desert.

▼ A Kumeyaay leader wears a ceremonial headdress.

The Kumeyaay land was divided into regions. Each region had a general who led the bands that lived there. Each band had a leader called a captain. Each captain had a **council**. A council is a group of people who help a leader make decisions. The leader and his council lived in a central village. They held important **ceremonies** in the village. A ceremony is a special way to do something to mark an important time.

120

The **shaman** was an important member of the council. A shaman was a religious leader who led the shaman ceremonies. If a child was "called to" be a shaman, the child was taught prayers, songs, and knowledge. The council also included healers. They used medicines from plants and herbs. They also used special songs.

▲ Plumes of eagle feathers were part of some Kumeyaay ceremonies.

The Kumeyaay had ceremonies for important events. The shaman decided the best time for each ceremony. There were ceremonies when girls and boys became adults. There were ceremonies for marriages, to name babies, and to honor the dead. Ceremonies included singing, dancing, drumming, and storytelling. They also used songs and dances to pray for hunting and health.

Five Kumeyaay elders lead a ceremony. ▶

THE KARUK TRIBE
OF NORTHERN CALIFORNIA

▲ Mount Shasta

The History of the Karuk Tribe

Native Americans have lived in California for thousands of years. The Karuk (Karok) Tribe had about 1200 members when Europeans arrived in the 1700s. This tribe lived in the Klamath River valley near Mount Shasta. Their land had many mountains and fresh water.

California's northern rain forest was a good place to hunt and fish. The Karuk (Karok) had villages among the rivers, lagoons, and bays. They used dugout canoes to travel up and down the Klamath River. The canoes were made from redwood trees.

◀ A Karuk woman in 1924

Tribal elders led the tribe. They decided who fished and hunted on their land. The Karuk (Karok) had slaves from conquered tribes.

Mount Shasta, in northern California, was sacred to the Karuk (Karok). They held the World Renewal Ceremony there. This ceremony happened each fall. The people prepared by washing in the rivers. They danced and prayed. This ceremony was held to prevent earthquakes, floods, and crop failures.

The Karuk Tribe Now

Today, the Karuk (Karok) tribe still lives near Mount Shasta. The people have changed, but they still hunt and fish. They still make beautiful baskets and other artwork. They still have World Renewal at Mount Shasta. Most important, they protect the land. They work to keep Mount Shasta and the Klamath River clean.

For many years, the Karuk (Karok) people were made to live in a small reservation. They did not have the same rights as most Americans. Today, the Karuk (Karok) people work with the U.S. Forest Service to protect the land. The Forest Service learns about land management from the Karuk (Karok). —*Lisa Jo Rudy*

▼ A Karuk woman and her child in 2007

Cause/Effect Writing Frame

Use the Writing Frame to orally summarize "Leadership of the Kumeyaay."

Because the Kumeyaay had many people and covered a large

territory, they made _____ .

The **effect** of this was that each region had a general who _____

_____ .

The Kumeyaay also had councils that _____

_____ .

A shaman was an important member of a council **because**

he or she _____ .

If a child had a special call to be a shaman, **then** he or she _____

_____ .

Because the Kumeyaay had ceremonies for important events,

the shaman decided _____

_____ .

Use the Writing Frame to write the summary on another sheet of paper. Be sure to include the **bold** signal words. Keep this as a model of this Text Structure.

Critical Thinking

1   A group of people who led a community, state, or nation is called a _____.

    A. shaman

    B. gathering

    C. government

2   Point to the sentences in "The Karuk Tribe of Northern California" that tell you about the canoes of the Karuk (Karok).

3   Work with a partner to find information about the World Renewal Ceremony in "The Karuk Tribe of Northern California."

4   Read aloud the caption for the photograph of the Kumeyaay leader on page 120. What does the caption tell you about the photograph?

> A caption is an explanation of a photograph.

Digital Learning

For a list of links and activities that relate to this History/Social Studies standard, visit the California Treasures Web site at www.macmillanmh.com to access the Content Reader resources. Have students watch the video "Native American Communities." In addition, distribute copies of the Translated Concept Summaries in Spanish, Chinese, Hmong, Khmer, and Vietnamese.

CALIFORNIA COMMUNITIES

NEWCOMERS BRING CHANGE

In 1492 Christopher Columbus sailed to North America. About 50 years later, Spanish **explorers** sailed up what is now the California coast. Explorers are people who go to a place that is new to them to find out about it.

The Kawaiisu, the Hupa, the Kumeyaay, and other Native American groups had been living in California for thousands of years. Life changed for these Native Americans once Spanish settlers came. The newcomers took the land. The Native Americans fought back, but the newcomers had better weapons. The newcomers brought diseases that the Native Americans had never had—such as smallpox or measles. Many Native Americans died.

▲ A Spanish soldier around the year 1790

▼ Some Kumeyaay Native Americans lived and worked at Spanish settlements.

By the early 1900s most Native American groups had lost their homelands. Some lived on **reservations**. A reservation is land the United States government gives to Native Americans. However, in California, most Native American groups were not given reservations.

The Hupa kept much of their original homeland. Instead of only hunting and fishing, many began to farm. Today the Hupa earn money through logging and selling wood from their forest homeland.

▲ A Hupa woman making a basket

The Spanish settled on Kumeyaay lands on the coast. They forced the Native Americans to leave their winter homes and stay in the mountains all year. More and more settlers came to California when it became part of the United States. The Kumeyaay lost more land. They lost their rights and were treated unfairly.

Hupa logging on their reservation ▶

Welcome to the
National Museum
OF THE
American
INDIAN

Michael Ventura/Alamy

A museum opened in Washington, D.C., in 2004. It is the National Museum of the American Indian. A member of the Blackfoot tribe helped to design it. It looks like a landform in the Southwest desert.

A Collector

Not everything in the museum was collected by American Indians. George Heye collected many of the objects in the museum. Heye was not a Native American.

George Heye was born in 1874. His father made a lot of money by drilling oil on Native American land. George became interested in Native American people and customs. He started buying Native American items when he was in college. He bought items from different tribes. After 60 years, he owned 800,000 Native American items.

Werner Forman/Topham/The Image Works

▲ Native Americans made this neck ornament more than 1,000 years ago. It was found in Tennessee.

Werner Forman/Corbis Images

▲ Native Americans of the Northwest Coast made this headdress.

Heye's collection is now a big part of the National Museum of the American Indian. Native American people run the museum. They decide what to put in the galleries. They decide how their stories should be told.

The museum tells a story that started 10,000 years ago. The story tells about Native American lives, beliefs, and people. Over time, each tribe will tell its own story.

The Pomo Indian People

The Pomo are Native Americans. Their story—and the stories of all Native Americans—will be told in the museum.

The Pomo people lived all over California. They hunted, fished, and gathered fruits and nuts. The Pomo were peaceful people.

The Pomo made friends with Russians when they came to California. Later, the Pomo suffered from diseases such as smallpox. They got these diseases from the Russians.

▲ Pomo Indians Chief Little John, 110 years old, and his great grandson Little Eagle Feather, 1933

Raiders captured many Pomo and forced them into slavery.

Today the Pomo own only 50 acres of land in Northern California. But there are 75 Pomo tribes. All of the tribes are famous for their beautiful baskets and artwork. —*Lisa Jo Rudy*

▼ Pomo baskets

Sequence Writing Frame

Use the Writing Frame to orally summarize "Newcomers Bring Change."

The Kawaiisu, the Hupa, the Kumeyaay, and other Native American groups lived in California for thousands of years. **Then,**

in 1492, _____

_____ .

About 50 years **later,** _____

_____ .

After Spanish settlers came, _____

_____ .

After the Spanish settled on Kumeyaay they forced _____

_____ .

When California became part of the United States, _____

_____ .

Use the Writing Frame to write the summary on another sheet of paper. Be sure to include the **bold** signal word. Keep this as a model for writing a summary of this Text Structure.

Critical Thinking

1 People who go to a place that is new to them to find out about it are called _____.

    A. explorers

    B. groups

    C. nutrients

2 Revisit "Welcome to the National Museum of the American Indian." Why is George Heye's collection of Native American items important?

3 Point out three facts in "Welcome to the National Museum of the American Indian" about the Pomo Indian people.

4 Discuss with a partner how the photograph of the men logging on page 127 supports the text in "Newcomers Bring Change."

A photograph is a picture taken with a camera.

Digital Learning

For a list of links and activities that relate to this History/Social Science standard, visit the California Treasures Web site at www.macmillanmh.com to access the Content Reader resources. Have students watch the video "Native American Communities." In addition, distribute copies of the Translated Concept Summaries in Spanish, Chinese, Hmong, Khmer, and Vietnamese.

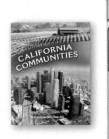

CALIFORNIA COMMUNITIES

TOWNS WITH A SPANISH BACKGROUND

How did your community begin? Many towns in California have names that begin with *San* or *Santa*. These places may have been settled by the Spanish. Today there are many places in California with a Spanish **heritage**. *Heritage* means "something handed down from the past."

Spanish explorers claimed California for Spain. Juan Rodríguez Cabrillo was the first to explore the California coast in 1542. Sixty years later, Sebastián Vizcaíno survived a terrible storm that almost sank his ships. He sailed to safety into an area that he named Santa Barbara.

Spanish settlers built settlements and missions. A **mission** is a settlement built around a church. In 1786 Spanish settlers founded Mission Santa Barbara.

Explorers and Founders

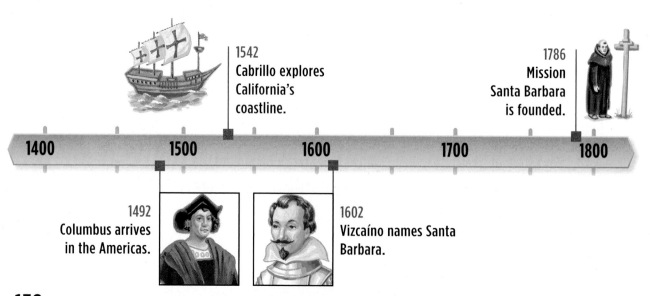

1542
Cabrillo explores California's coastline.

1786
Mission Santa Barbara is founded.

1400   1500   1600   1700   1800

1492
Columbus arrives in the Americas.

1602
Vizcaíno names Santa Barbara.

NEW PEOPLE, NEW TOWNS

After 1848 people rushed to California from around the world to find gold. People started mining camps and towns.

Years later, during the 1940s, many people began to **migrate**, or move, to California from other parts of the United States. **Developments**, or groups of houses, were built for them. Today new families from Latin America and Asia have moved into these developments. They brought their cultures with them.

▲ Lakewood, California, a planned development

▼ Philip Choy (far left), age six, with his family in 1932

Some families came to California from far away. Philip Choy's family came from China. Philip went to a public school when he was a boy. He also went to another school to learn his Chinese culture. Today his grandchildren learn the Chinese language and culture.

▼ The Choy family today

American Dreams

People come to the United States from around the world. They may not speak good English at first. They may have little education. Some of them sew clothes, or pick fruit or do other jobs that require few skills. In time many immigrants start their own businesses.

Find the American Dream

Many people from India have gone into the hotel business. People from Korea make clothes or sell groceries. Many people from Mexico came to pick fruit. Now they own farms and vineyards. At first, these businesses are small, but enough to make a living. Even the children work. Many of those children go to college when they grow up.

David Frasier/Photo Edit

▲ **This immigrant woman picks fruit to earn money.**

Spencer Grant/Photo Edit

This immigrant family owns a store. ▶

They Come Home to the Family Business

In the past, many of the children of immigrants were not interested in their families' businesses. Now grown children of immigrants want to come back. Many of them have good ideas. They can make their parents' businesses better.

Peter Kim and his father

Stephanie Diani

Peter Kim is a Korean American from southern California. He went back to help with his father's failing clothing business. He turned the company into a big success with his new ideas.

Priti Patel's family came from India. She counted change and worked the front desk at age 8. "I used to hate it," she says. "Everybody else gets to go home after school and get a snack. I had to help at the hotel. On weekends I had to cut grass." She felt embarrassed when friends saw her working. Later, though, Patel earned a business degree. Today she runs one of her family's motels.

Citizenship: the true American dream

AP Photo/Nick Ut

These Americans build on the American dreams their parents worked so hard for.

Sequence Writing Frame

**Use the Writing Frame to orally summarize
"Towns with a Spanish Background."**

The **first** person from Spain to explore California, in 1542, was

_____ .

Sixty years **later**, _____
explored California's coast.

A terrible storm almost sank his ships. Then he sailed safely

in an area he named _____ .

Later, in 1786, Spanish settlers _____

_____ .

Today there are many places in California with _____ .

After 1848, people _____ .

Then, during the 1940s, many people began to _____

_____ from other parts of the United States.

Today new families from _____ .

Use the Writing Frame to write the summary on another sheet
of paper. Be sure to include the **bold** signal words. Keep this as
a model of this Text Structure.

Critical Thinking

1 _____ means something handed down from the past.

    A. Mission

    B. House

    C. Heritage

2 Revisit "American Dreams" and tell what some people from different countries may do to earn money in the United States.

3 Find the paragraph in "American Dreams" that tells about Priti Patel. Describe her situation to a partner.

4 Discuss the time line on page 132 with a partner.

A time line is a line of significant events in a subject area.

Digital Learning

For a list of links and activities that relate to this History/Social Science standard, visit the California Treasures Web site at www.macmillanmh.com to access the Content Reader resources. Have students view the video "Communities Change."
In addition, distribute copies of the Translated Concept Summaries in Spanish, Chinese, Hmong, Khmer, and Vietnamese.

A GOLD RUSH TOWN

When gold was discovered in California, people came by the thousands. They hoped to get rich. Miners had to get **claims**. A claim is a legal right to mine on a certain area of land. Often there were no rules or police. Miners sometimes made their own rules to protect their claims.

The miners needed to eat. They needed their laundry cleaned, too. Some people started businesses instead of digging for gold. They sold hardware or ran hotels or restaurants. Some people got rich from gold during the Gold Rush. More people got rich by selling goods and services.

▼ Gold miners visited barber shops to get shaves.

San Francisco grew from a tiny settlement into a large city. Ships carrying gold seekers arrived during the Gold Rush. Some of the ships were sunk in the harbor after these people left the ships to find gold. People added dirt and stones to the harbor to make **landfill**. Landfill is dry land that people make by filling in areas of water. Today some of San Francisco stands on landfill.

Spanish settlers founded many towns and cities in California. People from other countries such as China also settled in gold-mining towns during the Gold Rush. They started businesses. In time, small towns grew and developed. Many years later, Vietnamese people came to California to escape a war in Vietnam. Seema Handu and her husband came from India. "We love that there are people here from many different countries."

San Francisco, 1850–2000

PACIFIC OCEAN

San Francisco Bay

N S E W

- ■ Built-up area, 1850
- ■ Built-up area, 1900
- ■ Built-up area, 1950
- ☐ Built-up area, 2000
- ☐ Landfill to 1900
- ▨ Landfill 1900–2000
- ☐ Parks

0   2   4 miles
0   2   4 kilometers

▲ How did San Francisco change over time?

▼ Immigrants and their families help California towns and cities grow.

A Magnificent Collection

▲ **Mayme Clayton**

Mayme Clayton collected books, magazines, and letters written by African Americans. The books were rare and hard to find. They were written by authors who helped create African American culture.

Phillis Wheatley wrote one book in the collection. Wheatley was a slave who wrote poetry. She was the first African American to publish a book. The book was signed by Wheatley. No one else owns a copy signed by Phillis Wheatley.

Mrs. Clayton died at age 83. By then, she had over 30,000 books by or about African Americans. Her collection also includes papers about slaves, photographs, movies, and sheet music. It is one of the biggest private collections of African American history and culture in the United States.

POEMS
ON
VARIOUS SUBJECTS,
RELIGIOUS AND MORAL.
BY
PHILLIS WHEATLEY,
NEGRO SERVANT to Mr. JOHN WHEATLEY,
of BOSTON, in NEW ENGLAND.

LONDON,
Printed for A. BELL, Bookseller, Aldgate;
Messrs. COX and BERRY, King-Street, BOSTON.
MDCCLXXIII.

▲ **The only known signed copy of Phillis Wheatley's book**

Her son, Avery Clayton, wanted to set up a museum for his mother's collection. The collection's new home will probably be in Culver City, California. Avery Clayton especially wants kids to see the collection. "African American culture is currently being defined by pop culture," he says. "It's important to offer a more complete picture."

Scholars say that Mrs. Clayton's collection is extremely important. She did this work so part of African American heritage was not lost. "We didn't know these things existed," says Sara Hodson of California's Huntington Library. —*Kathryn Satterfield*

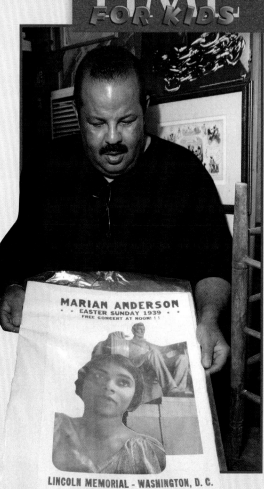

Melissa Roth/The New York Times/Redux

▲ **Avery Clayton with a poster from his mother's collection**

Courtesy of Avery Clayton

◄ **These books make Mrs. Clayton's collection extremely important.**

Compare/Contrast Writing Frame

Use the Writing Frame to orally summarize "A Gold Rush Town."

Each period of settlement in California was a little different.

Miners during the Gold Rush had claims, or a legal _____

_____ .

However, miners made _____ .

Some people got rich from gold, **but** more people got rich by _____

_____ .

When gold seekers arrived in San Francisco, it was only a _____

_____ .

However, it grew into a _____ .

In the beginning, Spanish settlers in California founded _____

_____ .

But then, during the Gold Rush, people from _____

_____ .

Use the Writing Frame to write the summary on another sheet of paper. Be sure to include the **bold** signal words. Keep this as a model of this Text Structure.

Critical Thinking

1   Dry land that people make by filling in areas of water is
    called _____.

    A. landfill

    B. laundry

    C. large city

2   Point out the sentences in "A Magnificent Collection" that
    explain what Mayme Clayton did.

3   Read aloud the text in this article that tells why Mrs. Clayton's
    collection is extremely important.

4   Describe for a partner the map on page 139.

    A map is a drawing
    that shows where different
    places are.

Digital Learning

For a list of links and activities that relate to this History/Social
Science standard, visit the California Treasures Web site at
www.macmillanmh.com to access the Content Reader resources.
Have students view the video "Communities Change."
In addition, distribute copies of the Translated Concept Summaries in
Spanish, Chinese, Hmong, Khmer, and Vietnamese.

RULES AND LAWS PROTECT EVERYONE

Communities and countries need rules. A rule that is made by a government for people in a community is called a **law**. Some laws help keep people safe, such as laws that tell drivers how fast to drive. Some laws protect property. Laws say that no one may break into a home or steal from a home. People who break laws are punished. They may have to pay money or go to jail.

Our government follows rules, too. Some of the most important rules the government must follow are in the United States Constitution. A constitution is a plan for government. Our country's Constitution was written more than 200 years ago. It says what our government can and cannot do. The people we elect promise to obey the Constitution.

Rules and laws protect people at the beach. ▶

BEACH RULES
- **NO SWIMMING BEYOND THE SWIM LINE. ALL SWIMMERS MUST STAY WITHIN THE DESIGNATED SWIM AREAS.**
- **ALCOHOLIC BEVERAGES ARE PROHIBITED.**
- **PLEASE DO NOT THROW STONES OR ROCKS.**

We the People *of the United States, in order to form a more perfect Union, establish Justice, insure domestic Tranquility, provide for the common Defence, promote the general Welfare, and secure the Blessings of Liberty to ourselves and our Posterity, do ordain and establish this Constitution for the United States of America.*

▲ The United States Constitution begins with the words "We the People."

Good citizens follow rules and laws. Good citizens believe in the **common good**. *Common good* means "doing what is best for everyone." Good citizens know that rules and laws protect everyone.

You can help out at your school or in your community. You are a good citizen if you read to younger children at a school, help others in the classroom, pick up trash, or collect cans for a food drive.

You can get involved in school government. This is another way to help your school community. You can stay involved with government as you grow up. You can work to improve schools.

Voting is a responsibility of good citizens. When people vote, they make decisions about laws and who they want in government.

Good citizens help others. ▶

Teens to the Rescue!

LEGO

Post 53 EMTs,
left to right: Wells
Landers, 18; Kate
Kevorkian, 17;
Annie Maybell, 17;
Emily Stout, 17

Emily Stout and the other emergency medical technicians (EMTs) jumped out of their ambulance on I-95 in Darien, Connecticut. A man was slumped against a concrete barrier. His leg was bloody. His crushed car lay a few feet away.

The team quickly put a collar on the man to protect his neck. They bandaged his leg, and lifted him onto a stretcher and into the ambulance. They raced off to a nearby hospital. Then they wheeled him into the emergency room.

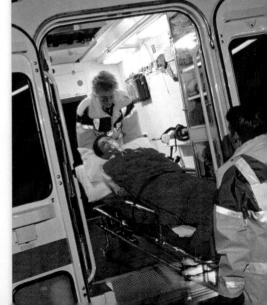

Chris Baker/Stone/Getty Images

EMTs at work ▶

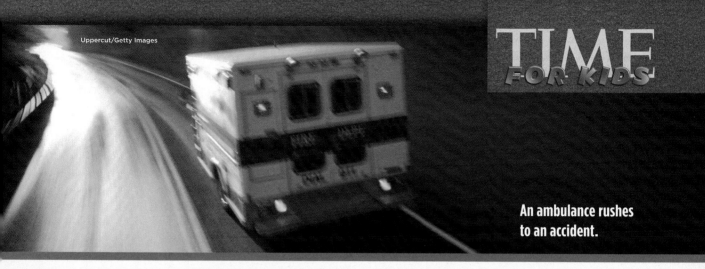

Uppercut/Getty Images

An ambulance rushes to an accident.

Emily and 58 other teens volunteer for the Darien Emergency Medical Service. Their service is called Post 53. It is Darien's only ambulance service.

These teens take about 1,450 calls each year. They respond to car crashes and heart attacks and help deliver babies. Trained adults help them. "I've had cases where patients wouldn't have lived without them," says Timothy S. Hall, Stamford Hospital's chairman of surgery.

Post 53 was started in 1969. Teens who join the team must pass a screening, do 140 hours of training, and pass an exam. Then they become certified emergency medical technicians.

They are on call 120 hours a month. They carry radio transmitters everywhere, even to class. They stop what they are doing when they are called.

"Once, I had to leave three minutes before *Harry Potter* ended," Emily Stout says. All the work is worth it. Just ask Jim Cloud. Cloud's heart stopped, but the teens started it again. Jim's wife says: "They saved his life. They're magnificent." —*Molly Lopez*

Dr. Timothy Hall says the teens saved the lives of some of his patients. ▶

Courtesy of Stamford Hospital

147

Description Writing Frame

Use the Writing Frame to orally summarize "Rules and Laws Protect Everyone."

Communities and countries need rules. Some laws, **for example**,

tell drivers _____ .

Others laws protect property. Laws **such as** these say that _____

_____ .

Our government follows rules, too. Some of **the most important**

rules are in _____ .

Following rules and laws is part of being a _____ .

Good citizens believe in the _____

_____ .

Good citizens know that _____

_____ .

Good citizens do things **such as** _____

_____ .

Use the Writing Frame to write the summary on another sheet
of paper. Be sure to include the **bold** signal words. Keep this as
a model of this Text Structure.

Critical Thinking

1   A rule that is made by a government for people in a community is called a _____.

   A. responsibility

   B. plan

   C. law

2   Point to the sentences in "Teens to the Rescue!" that tell how some teens from Post 53 help others.

3   Read aloud the text that tells what teens do to join Post 53.

4   Talk about the Constitution with a partner. What does the caption tell you about the photograph on page 145?

> A caption is an explanation of a photograph.

Digital Learning

For a list of links and activities that relate to this History/Social Science standard, visit the California Treasures Web site at www.macmillanmh.com to access the Content Reader resources. Have students view the video "Many Communities, One Nation." In addition, distribute copies of the Translated Concept Summaries in Spanish, Chinese, Hmong, Khmer, and Vietnamese.

SYMBOLS OF OUR COUNTRY

The bald eagle is our national bird. Its strength and independence represent the strength and freedom of the United States.

The American flag is a **symbol** of our country. A symbol is something that stands for or represents something else. The stars of our flag stand for the 50 states. The stripes stand for the original 13 colonies.

The Statue of Liberty is another symbol. **Liberty** means "freedom from control by someone else." The Statue of Liberty symbolizes our country's freedom.

The Declaration of Independence is the document that explained to the world why the United States wanted to be free and independent. We remember the ideas of freedom when we see it.

Symbols remind us of important ideas. ▼

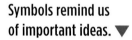

Local Landmarks and Symbols

Communities can have important symbols. They can also have landmarks. Landmarks are objects or places that have a special importance. These symbols and landmarks tell us about the history of our communities. They also tell us what our communities think is important.

The city seal of Oakland, California, honors one of its landmarks. This landmark is the large oak tree in front of City Hall. The oak tree is a symbol of strength. It also reminds people of Oakland's natural beauty and resources.

This is the California State Seal. The word *Eureka* reminds us of the discovery of gold.

Symbols remind us of important ideas.

▼ The oak tree is a symbol of Oakland.

Open Liberty!

Thousands of visitors come to see the Statue of Liberty every year. For over 100 years, they were allowed to enter and climb 354 steps to the crown.

Everything changed on September 11, 2001. The statue and its grounds on Liberty Island were closed to visitors after the terrorist attacks. Officials worried that the site was not safe. The island reopened three months later, but the statue remained closed.

Finally, officials allowed visitors to enter the statue in the summer of 2004. However, tourists can only climb to the top of the statue's pedestal.

A Towering Symbol

The Statue of Liberty came to the United States in 1885. It was a gift from the people of France. It recognized the friendship between the countries during the American Revolution.

The head of the Statue of Liberty in Paris, France, 1883 ▶

Around 1900

Archive Holdings Inc./Getty Images

Today

WizData, inc./Alamy

The statue became a symbol of freedom and democracy. Immigrants saw it and knew they were safe and free.

Now visitors must call first to get into the Statue of Liberty. They must go through security systems. It is better than not getting in at all.

U.S. Representative Anthony Weiner of New York hopes tourists will one day be allowed to climb the statue. "Reopening the statue can mean only one thing: reopening all of it."

Charlie DeLeo, Keeper of the Flame

Charlie DeLeo is a volunteer who has worked inside the Statue of Liberty for over 30 years. He has made about 2,500 trips to the statue's flame. He goes up to the top of her torch every month. There, he replaces burned-out lights and removes bird droppings.

Courtesy of Charlie DeLeo

153

Compare/Contrast Writing Frame

Use the Writing Frame to orally summarize "Symbols of Our Country."

The symbols of our country are **similar** but also **different**. The

bald eagle is **like** the American flag because _____

_____.

But the bald eagle is _____.

Unlike the bald eagle, the stars and stripes of our flag stand for _____

_____.

Like the eagle and the American flag, the Statue of Liberty is a _____

_____.

The eagle and the Statue of Liberty **both** stand for _____.

The Declaration of Independence is **different** from the other

symbols because it is a _____.

Use the Writing Frame to write the summary on another sheet of paper. Be sure to include the **bold** symbol words. Keep this as a model of this Text Structure.

Critical Thinking

1   Freedom from control by someone else is called _____.

    A. strength

    B. liberty

    C. landmark

2   Point out the sentence in "Open Liberty!" that explains what the Statue of Liberty symbolizes.

3   Find the paragraph about Charlie DeLeo. Why is he called "Keeper of the Flame"?

4   Discuss with a small group the photograph of the Great Seal of the State of California on page 151. What does the word *Eureka* remind people of?

> A photograph is a picture taken with a camera.

Digital Learning

For a list of links and activities that relate to this History/Social Science standard, visit the California Treasures Web site at www.macmillanmh.com to access the Content Reader resources. Have students visit the Field Trip "Washington, D.C." In addition, distribute copies of the Translated Concept Summaries in Spanish, Chinese, Hmong, Khmer, and Vietnamese.

PARTS OF OUR GOVERNMENT

The Constitution divides the United States government into three parts, or branches. Congress is the **legislative** branch. It writes our laws. The **executive** branch makes sure people follow the laws. The President of the United States leads the executive branch. The third branch is the **judicial** branch, or our courts. The courts decide what the laws mean. They make sure the laws follow the Constitution.

California's state government also has three branches. The state assembly and the state senate make up the legislative branch. They make laws. The head of a state's executive branch is the **governor**. The judicial branch reviews state laws to see if they are fair.

Local government makes the decisions that affect a town or a city. There is often a **city council**. This is the legislative branch. It makes the laws. The **mayor** is the head of the city council. Citizens of the area vote for the mayor and the city council members.

◀ The California State Seal is a symbol of its government.

▼ Congress is the legislative branch. It makes laws for our country.

California, Native American Governments, and the United States

California sends lawmakers to Congress. It pays taxes to the federal, or national, government. Every state does these things.

All states, including California, send representatives to Congress. These people represent the state. Congress has two parts, or houses. The Senate has 100 members, two for each state. The House of Representatives has 435 members. States with more people get to have more representatives.

Native Americans are citizens of the United States. However, they are also citizens of their tribes. Many tribes have their own governments. They elect their own leaders and make their own laws. They also follow local, state, and national laws.

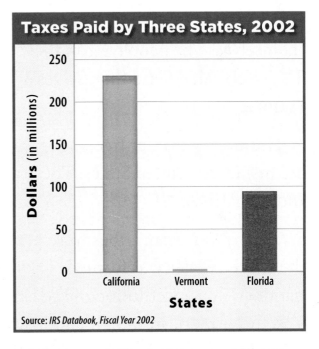

Taxes Paid by Three States, 2002

Dollars (in millions)

Source: *IRS Databook, Fiscal Year 2002*

Tribal leaders and local leaders work together to solve problems. ▼

 This graph compares California's taxes with the taxes of two other states.

American Indian Nations

The United States is a free, independent country. It is a nation. Its people govern themselves. The people make their own laws. They also can defend themselves against other nations.

The U.S. Capitol

Hundreds of other free, independent nations are inside the United States. These are American Indian nations.

Native American tribes were nations before the United States was formed. They are still nations. The Constitution of the United States says that American Indian nations and the United States should accept each other as nations.

Chippewa-Cree powwow at the Rocky Boy Reservation in Montana

The United States does not have to accept every group of Native Americans as a nation. There is a long process to decide which groups are nations. It can take years for the United States to accept a group of Native Americans as a nation.

To be accepted as a nation, the group of Native Americans must show that the group existed before the United States started. The group may also have to show that it has signed treaties that were accepted by the United States government.

Once a group of Native Americans is accepted as a sovereign, or self-governing, nation, it gains many rights. These include

- the right to make its own government

- the right to decide who is part of its sovereign nation

- the right to manage relations among its members

- the right to decide who inherits what

- the right to tax members and nonmembers who do business with members

- the right to use and give or sell land

- the right to make laws

American Indian nations have many rights and limits. For example, they cannot put a non-Native American in jail. —*Lisa Jo Rudy*

Bettmann/Corbis

▲ The U.S. government and the Lakota sign a treaty in Wyoming, 1868.

Flags of two nations: American and Santa Ynez Band of Chumash Indians ▶

Marilyn Angel Wynn/Nativestock/Corbis

Narragansett Indian Tribal Police, Rhode Island ▶

Victoria Arocho/AP Photo

159

Cause/Effect Writing Frame

**Use the Writing Frame to orally summarize
"Parts of Our Government."**

One **result** of the U.S. Constitution is that the United States

government has _____.

The job of the executive branch is to make sure laws are
followed. **Since** the President of the United States is the leader

of our country, the President _____.

Because the judicial branch includes our court system, _____

_____.

A legislative branch writes laws. **Therefore**, California's laws are

made by the _____.

The judicial branch includes the courts. This means that the

California judicial branch reviews _____.

Since local governments make the decisions that affect a town

or city, they need a _____,

which is the _____.

Use the Writing Frame to write the summary on another sheet
of paper. Be sure to include the **bold** signal words. Keep this as
a model for writing a summary of this Text Structure.

Critical Thinking

1   The head of the state's executive branch is
the _____ .

   A. mayor

   B. president

   C. governor

2   Find the paragraph in "American Indian Nations" that
describes what the Constitution says about Indian
nations and the United States.

3   Reread in "American Indian Nations" the list of rights for
a group of Indians accepted as a sovereign nation.
Which rights do you think are most important?
Why?

4   Point out the bar graph on page 157. Discuss it
with a partner.

A bar graph is a
drawing with bars
whose lengths represent
amounts.

Digital Learning

For a list of links and activities that relate to this History/Social
Science standard, visit the California Treasures Web site at
www.macmillanmh.com to access the Content Reader resources.
Have students view the video "Many Communities, One Nation."
In addition, distribute copies of the Translated Concept Summaries in
Spanish, Chinese, Hmong, Khmer, and Vietnamese.

CALIFORNIA COMMUNITIES

FIGHTERS FOR FREEDOM

Anne Hutchinson was an American who believed in freedom of religion. Freedom of religion is the right to practice any religion you choose or no religion at all. Anne was born in England. She came to North America with her family in 1634. Her father taught her to think for herself. He told her to express her thoughts.

Anne was very religious. She invited people to her home to talk about religion. Her beliefs were different from the beliefs of the ministers of her community. Anne was arrested and put on trial for her beliefs. The court ordered Anne to leave the community. She left, but she never gave up her right to have her own beliefs.

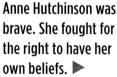
Anne Hutchinson was brave. She fought for the right to have her own beliefs. ▶

◀ Thomas Jefferson wrote most of the Declaration of Independence.

Benjamin Franklin fought for freedom and democracy. ▶

Thomas Jefferson and Benjamin Franklin were Americans who helped our country win independence from Great Britain. They were two of the men chosen in 1776 to write the Declaration of Independence. This document told Great Britain why Americans wanted to be free. Americans fought a long war to be free from Great Britain.

Jefferson wrote that "all men are created equal." However, **slavery** was legal in the colonies. Slavery is the practice of keeping people against their wills and forcing them to work. In 1783, our country won its freedom from Great Britain. Franklin asked Congress to end slavery. Congress refused.

Thomas Jefferson

Thomas Jefferson had a lot of jobs.

Thomas Jefferson was a busy man. He wrote most of the Declaration of Independence. Later, he was President of the United States. He was also a farmer, a writer, and an inventor.

Thomas Jefferson was born in 1743 to wealthy parents. He grew up on a plantation in Virginia. Jefferson trained to be a lawyer, but became a politician.

In 1776 Jefferson was in Philadelphia. He was one of Virginia's representatives to Congress. That's when he wrote most of the Declaration of Independence. This declaration was the battle cry of the revolution against the British.

Thomas Jefferson (left) and others worked on the Declaration of Independence. ▶

The Granger Collection, New York

The Granger Collection, New York

Monticello

Jefferson was elected governor of Virginia in 1779. In 1785 he became an ambassador to France. He became vice president of the United States in 1796. He became President in 1800.

Jefferson did not like big government. All the same, he made the Louisiana Purchase. He bought an amount of land that doubled the size of the United States. The Louisiana Purchase was as big as the rest of the United States.

Jefferson said he did not want a permanent army. All the same, he started the U.S. Marines.

Jefferson wrote in the Declaration of Independence that all men are created equal. However, Jefferson owned slaves. He did nothing to end slavery when he was President.

Jefferson returned to Virginia after his second term as President. There, in his home called Monticello, he designed the University of Virginia. He also wrote, invented new tools, and relaxed. —Lisa Jo Rudy

Jefferson's plan for the University of Virginia.

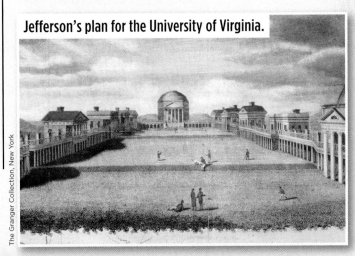

Compare/Contrast Writing Frame

Use the Writing Frame to orally summarize "Fighters for Freedom."

Anne Hutchinson was an American who met with people to talk

about religion. **However**, her ideas were _____

_____ .

Because her ideas were **in contrast** to other peoples' ideas, she

was _____ .

Thomas Jefferson and Benjamin Franklin were both _____

_____ .

Both of these men were chosen in 1776 to _____ .

This document told _____ .

Jefferson wrote that "all men are created equal." **However**, slavery was

_____ .

In 1789, Benjamin Franklin wanted Congress to end slavery.

Unlike Franklin, **however**, Congress did not want _____ .

Use the Writing Frame to write the summary on another sheet
of paper. Be sure to include the **bold** signal words. Keep this as
a model of this Text Structure.

Critical Thinking

1. The practice of keeping people and forcing them to work is called _____.

    A. independence

    B. bravery

    C. slavery

2. Reread the sentences in "Thomas Jefferson" about Thomas Jefferson's jobs. Name two of these jobs.

3. Point to the sentence in "Thomas Jefferson" that states when Thomas Jefferson became President of the United States.

4. With a partner, compare and contrast the pictures and the captions on pages 162 and 163.

A caption is an explanation of a photograph.

Digital Learning

For a list of links and activities that relate to this History/Social Science standard, visit the California Treasures Web site at www.macmillanmh.com to access the Content Reader resources. Have students view the video "Many Communities, One Nation." In addition, distribute copies of the Translated Concept Summaries in Spanish, Chinese, Hmong, Khmer, and Vietnamese.

CALIFORNIA COMMUNITIES

FREEDOM FOR ALL

We remember Harriet Tubman and Frederick Douglass as people who worked to free enslaved Africans. Harriet Tubman was born into slavery in the South. She escaped to the North, where she became free. For many years, she risked her life to lead enslaved people to freedom. The roads she followed and places where people hid were known as the **Underground Railroad**.

Frederick Douglass was also born into slavery. As a young man, he escaped to the North. There he started a newspaper and wrote articles against slavery. He also traveled and gave speeches. Later he was an adviser to President Abraham Lincoln. Lincoln helped end slavery in the United States.

▲ Harriet Tubman worked to free enslaved people.

◄ Frederick Douglass also worked to free enslaved people.

Dr. Martin Luther King, Jr., worked for freedom and fairness. He spoke against **segregation**. Segregation is the separation of people by race or skin color. At one time, African Americans were not allowed to eat at the same restaurants or go to the same schools as whites. Dr. King asked government leaders for change. He led peaceful protests and marches, and refused to use violence.

▲ Dr. Martin Luther King, Jr., won the Nobel Peace Prize in 1964.

Elizabeth Cady Stanton and Susan B. Anthony worked for more than 50 years to gain equal rights for women in the United States. In 1851 women had few rights. In most places they could not own land. They could not vote. Stanton and Anthony wrote books, held meetings, and made speeches. They talked to Congress about rights for women.

▼ Susan B. Anthony

◀ Elizabeth Cady Stanton

Abraham Lincoln and Frederick Douglass

The Granger Collection, New York

Abraham Lincoln was President of the United States. Frederick Douglass was born into slavery. What did these two men have in common?

Both Lincoln and Douglass came from poor homes. Both men were big and tall. Both worked for the chance to learn to read and write. Both became wonderful writers and speakers. Both wanted to free enslaved people.

Frederick Douglass did not like Lincoln at first. Lincoln said he wanted to free enslaved people, but Douglass thought he was taking too long to do it.

Then, on New Year's Day 1863, Lincoln issued a statement. That statement, called the "Emancipation Proclamation," granted freedom to enslaved people in many Southern states. Soon Lincoln announced that black men could join the U.S. army. In 1865, slavery was ended in the United States.

Soon the two men became friends. They met at the White House.

Frederick Douglass came to the inauguration when Lincoln was elected President for the second time. There was a big party after Lincoln was sworn in. Policemen outside the White House tried to stop Douglass from entering. They said that no black men were invited. However, Lincoln said to let Douglass in.

"Here comes my friend," Lincoln said, and took Douglass by the hand. "I am glad to see you. I saw you in the crowd today, listening to my inaugural address." He asked Douglass how he liked it. Then Lincoln told Douglass, "There is no man in the country whose opinion I value more than yours." —*Lisa Jo Rudy*

The Granger Collection, New York

▲ President Lincoln greets guests at a reception after his second inauguration.

Bettmann/Corbis

▲ Lincoln reads the Emancipation Proclamation.

Compare/Contrast Writing Frame

**Use the Writing Frame to orally summarize
"Freedom for All."**

Both Harriet Tubman and Fredrick Douglass were born _____

_____ .

Unlike Frederick Douglass, Harriet Tubman risked her life to _____

_____ .

Like Harriet Tubman, Frederick Douglass was against _____

_____ .

Unlike Harriet Tubman, Frederick Douglass _____

_____ .

In the North, Douglass started a _____ .

Like Harriet Tubman and Frederick Douglass, Dr. Martin Luther

King, Jr., worked for _____ for African Americans.

In contrast, Elizabeth Cady Stanton and Susan B. Anthony worked

to gain rights for _____ .

Use the Writing Frame to write the summary on another sheet
of paper. Be sure to include the **bold** signal words. Keep it as a
model of this Text Structure.

Critical Thinking

1   The routes and places where slaves could hide on the way to freedom were called the _____.

    A. Congress

    B. Underground Railroad

    C. United States

2   Find the sentences in "Abraham Lincoln and Frederick Douglass" that tell how Lincoln and Douglass were alike.

3   Point out the text in "Abraham Lincoln and Frederick Douglass" that tells what the Emancipation Proclamation said.

4   Identify the photographs of Harriet Tubman, Frederick Douglass, and Martin Luther King, Jr., on pages 168 and 169. Discuss what these people did.

A photograph is a picture taken with a camera.

Digital Learning

For a list of links and activities that relate to this History/Social Science standard, visit the California Treasures Web site at www.macmillanmh.com to access the Content Reader resources. Have students read the biography "Susan B. Anthony."
In addition, distribute copies of the Translated Concept Summaries in Spanish, Chinese, Hmong, Khmer, and Vietnamese.

FARMS IN CALIFORNIA

Many people in California earn money from agriculture. Agriculture is the business of growing crops or raising animals for food. More food is grown in California than in any other state. California's farming region has rich soil and water. The summers are hot and dry. These natural resources are important for farms. This area is the perfect place to grow grapes, cotton, tomatoes, and many other crops.

Farms need **human resources** to help them grow crops or raise animals. Human resources are the people who work for a business, the owners and workers. Cher Sue and Bor Yang Lor own a small farm near Fresno. Their 13 children work with them on the farm to grow vegetables.

Bor Yang Lor and her daughter sell their vegetables in Aptos, California.

Children were important human resources on farms in the past. They had regular chores to do. They gave food and water to the animals. Children helped in the house, too. Many farm children went to school only when they did not have to plant or pick crops.

Capital resources are part of farming and other businesses. Capital resources are tools and machines people use to produce goods. Farmers in the past used capital resources such as horse-drawn machines. Today most farms in California use capital resources such as tractors and computers.

Some people work in businesses that provide services for farmers. Some people in the government help farmers learn what works best on farms in California climates. These people can also help solve other problems.

Tractors are capital resources.

Children helped process food, such as peaches.

Corn Turns into Gold

Royalty Free/Corbis

Farmers in the United States grow a lot of corn. In the past, corn was used mostly for food for people and animals. However, a few years ago, that changed.

Ethanol is a fuel that can be made from corn. It can replace gasoline in cars. Gasoline causes pollution when it burns. Ethanol causes much less pollution when it burns.

The U.S. government decided that farmers should grow some corn for ethanol. So, the government said it would pay more for ethanol corn than for food corn. This extra money is called a subsidy.

Some farmers, like Bill Couser of Iowa, are excited about the ethanol subsidy. Couser has started a business. His business produces corn for ethanol. Other farmers in Iowa bought shares in Couser's company. That means they make money when Couser and the company make money. Couser and the other farmers have made a lot of money from ethanol corn.

Matthew Staver/UPI/Landov

Ethanol causes less pollution.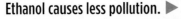

When farmers make money, the towns they live in make money, too. ▶

Farmers spend their money when they make money. The stores and businesses near the farmers make more money. The neighborhood gets richer.

However, Couser grows less corn for animal food when he grows corn for ethanol. Then, farmers who raise animals have to pay more for food corn. Now products made from the animals are more expensive to buy, too. Beef, which comes from cows, now costs more. Pork, chicken, and even eggs cost more.

▲ Expensive corn means expensive beef.

This change in the way we use corn raises the cost of many things. Popcorn costs more. The price of seed corn is higher. Farmers buy seed corn to grow corn. This higher price makes things difficult for families in the United States. In poorer countries, people may have nothing to eat if they cannot buy corn. —*Lisa Jo Rudy*

▲ A high price for corn is not good for people in poorer countries.

177

Problem/Solution Writing Frame

Use the Writing Frame to orally summarize "Farms in California."

In California, many people earn money from _____.

There are important natural resources for farming in California. There is a **problem** if farms do not also have

_____.

To solve this problem, people such as Cher Sue and Bor Yang

Lor, who own a small farm, have all their _____.

In the past, there was a **problem** when farms did not have enough

human resources. To solve this need, children worked by _____

_____.

Many farm children went to school only _____

_____.

Today, people on farms in California use capital resources such as

_____.

These things help **solve many problems** on farms.

Use the Writing Frame to write the summary on another sheet of paper. Be sure to include the **bold** signal words. Keep this as a model of this Text Structure.

Critical Thinking

1. The tools and machines people use to produce goods are called _____.

   A. children

   B. capital resources

   C. human resources

2. Show a partner the sentences in "Corn Turns into Gold" that describe ethanol.

3. Read aloud the text in "Corn Turns into Gold" that describes what happens when farmers make money.

4. Describe the photograph of the children with the peaches on page 175. Discuss with a partner what the caption tells you about this photograph.

> A caption is an explanation of a photograph.

Digital Learning

For a list of links and activities that relate to this History/Social Science standard, visit the California Treasures Web site at www.macmillanmh.com to access the Content Reader resources. Have students view the video "Communities at Work."

In addition, distribute copies of the Translated Concept Summaries in Spanish, Chinese, Hmong, Khmer, and Vietnamese.

CALIFORNIA COMMUNITIES

MADE IN CALIFORNIA

More products are made in California than in any other state in the country. Machines, clothes, toys, sports equipment, and other things are made in California's **factories**. A factory is a place where products are made.

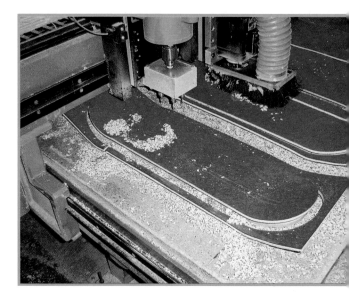

▲ Machines that cut wood into skateboard shapes are capital resources. The wood is a natural resourse.

Companies use natural resources, capital resources, and human resources to make products. For example, a skateboard company needs wood, a natural resource. The company needs machines to cut and shape the wood. The machines are capital resources. The people who make the skateboards are human resources.

Businesses try to buy their natural resources for low prices. Sometimes they can buy natural resources from local businesses. Other times they must buy them from elsewhere in the United States or other countries to get a lower price. A skateboard company in Santa Cruz, for example, may get wood from Canada.

▲ People who paint the skateboards are human resourses.

We Earn and Spend

People have jobs to earn **income**. Income is money received for work. The amount of income someone earns depends on the job he or she does. You work in school. You explore different subjects and learn many skills. What you do in school helps you prepare to earn an income one day.

Many people use a budget. A budget is a plan for using money. A budget shows how much money people have. It shows the ways that money can be spent. This helps them make smart spending choices.

Theo wants a new telescope to study the stars. His parents look at their budget. It shows their total income for the month. It shows how much money is for expenses. An expense is money spent to buy something. Theo's parents see if there is any money left to buy a telescope.

Family Budget	
Income	**Expenses**
Mom $1,756.00	**Needs**
	Groceries $375.00
Dad $2,170.00	Clothing $225.00
	Rent $1,400.00
	College fund $150.00
	Wants
	Fun things $100.00

▲ This is a budget for Theo's family.

Money

Parents want to teach their kids how to use money wisely. Most kids have a long list of things they want to spend their money on. Families need to find a balance between what parents and kids want.

You can mow lawns to earn money.

Peg Eddy tries to help people use their money wisely. Eddy and most experts think the best way for kids to learn is to have a little money of their own. Some parents give money to their kids. Some parents say kids must earn their money.

Ryan is 17 years old and lives in Denver, Colorado. His parents want him to earn the money for things he wants. He has done it! Ryan has mowed lawns since he was 8. Now he owns his own equipment. He has saved $7,800. He also bought a dirt bike and a sound system.

Save now . . .   . . . buy later!

Learn and Save

Money skills are important for success. David Brady helps children and young adults use their money wisely. He thinks they should learn how to earn, save, and invest.

Talk About It

Many kids want to learn how to use their money. They know that they may need it for college, which is expensive.

Parents may teach kids what they should not do. Experts say a positive message works better. Parents can help kids see that saving means thinking about the future. It means waiting for something that is important.

Kids can learn how to use money without harsh rules. Children can learn to make good rules for themselves as they make decisions about their money.

Description Writing Frame

Use the Writing Frame to orally summarize "Made in California."

Many interesting products are made in California.

For example, _____
are made in California factories.

Companies use three kinds of resources, which **include** _____

_____.

For instance, a skateboard company needs _____

_____.

The machines are **examples** of _____

_____.

The people who make the skateboards are **examples of**

_____.

Businesses might buy the natural resources they need from **such**

places as _____.

Use the Writing Frame to write the summary on another sheet of paper. Be sure to include the **bold** signal words. Keep this as a model of this Text Structure.

Critical Thinking

1 Money received from work is called _____.

   A. income

   B. expenses

   C. budget

2 Point out the sentences in "Money" that tell how Ryan earned money.

3 Reread "Money." How can children learn to use money wisely? Find the text that supports your answer.

4 Discuss the chart on page 181 with a partner. What information does it give?

> A chart is a drawing that shows information in the form of a table, graph, or picture.

Digital Learning

For a list of links and activities that relate to this History/Social Science standard, visit the California Treasures Web site at www.macmillanmh.com to access the Content Reader resources. Have students read the biography "César Chavez."
In addition, distribute copies of the Translated Concept Summaries in Spanish, Chinese, Hmong, Khmer, and Vietnamese.

Illustration Acknowledgements

54, 72, 90, 91(cr)(br): Tom Leonard. 78: Precision Graphics. 79: Vilma Ortiz-Dillon. 85, 91(b): Karen Minot. 132: Rich Stergulz

Photography Acknowledgements

All photos for Macmillan/McGraw-Hill except as noted below:

Cover: Alamy. 6: (tr) WoodyStock/Alamy; (br) Brian Pieters/Masterfile. 7: Alan Thornton/Stone/Getty Images. 12: Mauritius/age fotostock. 13: (cl) Lew Robertson/Food Pix/Jupiter Images; (br) Kevin Cruff/Taxi/Getty Images; (cr) Ian O'Leary/DK Images; (c) Madeline Polss/Envision. 18: (tr) C Squared Studios/Getty Images; (tr) V&A Images/Alamy; (tr) Stockbyte Silver/Alamy. 19: (b) Stocktrek/Brand X Pictures/Alamy; (cl) C Squared Studios/Getty Images. 24: Jim Cummins/Taxi/Getty Images. 25: (tr) David Keaton/CORBIS; (bl) Michael Keller/Index Stock. 30: (tr) Terry Oakley/Alamy; (b) David Muench/CORBIS. 31: (tl) David Fischer/Photodisc Red/Getty Images; (tr) Lisa Barber/Photonica/Getty Images. 36–37: DK Images (Dorling Kindersley Ltd.) Picture Library. 42: (tr) John Cancalosi/naturepl.com; (br) Richard Du Toit/naturepl.com. 43: (tr) Frank and Joyce Burek/PhotoDisc/Getty Images; (br) Owen Newman/naturepl.com. 48: (tr) Jay Syverson/CORBIS; (b) Danita Delimont/Alamy. 49: (cr) Paul Souders/The Image Bank/Getty Images; (br) Robert Harding Picture Library Ltd./Alamy. 60: (b) Ambient Images/Alamy. 61: Tom and Pat Leeson/Photo Researchers, Inc. 66: WorldFoto/Alamy. 67: (c) Steve Bloom Images/Alamy; (bl) Rod Patterson/ABPL/Animals Animals. 72: Peter Arnold, Inc./Alamy. 79: Comstock Images/Alamy. 96: (tr) Thomas Hallstein/Outsight Photography; (b) Bill Ross/CORBIS. 102: Robert Holmes/CORBIS. 103: Courtesy of The Department of Water and Power. 109: (br) A.W.Ericson/National Museum of the American Indian; (tcr) Denver Art Museum Collection: gift of Mrs. D. Bromfield. 114: American Museum of Natural History; (bl) Tim Street-Porter/Botanica. 115: California Academy of Science. 120: (cl) Terry W. Eggers/CORBIS; (br) San Diego Historical Society Davis Collection. 121: (tr) National Museum of the American Indian/Smithsonian Institution; (br) Edward H. Davis/The Constance DuBois Collection, San Diego Museum of Man. 126: Library of Congress. 127: (tr) Phoebe A. Hearst Museum of Anthropology; (b) Ed Kashi/CORBIS. 133: (tr) Jeff Gritchen; (b) Courtesy of the Choys; (cr) Courtesy of the Choys. 138: (b) courtesy of www.historichwy49.com; (tr) Courtesy of the Bancroft Library, University of California, Berkeley. 144: (b) Photo Edit; (tc) Joseph Sohm/ChromoSohm Inc./CORBIS; (cr) Photo Edit. 145: Bill Aron/PhotoEdit Inc. 150: Joseph Sohm/Visions of America/CORBIS. 151: (tl) One Mile Up Inc./Fotosearch; (cl) PhotoVault; (b) PhotoVault. 156: (b) Dennis Cook/AP WideWorld; (cl) One Mile Up, Inc./Fotosearch. 157: Ben Margot/AP Wideworld. 162: The Granger Collection. 163: (tl) The Granger Collection; (cr) Bettmann/CORBIS. 168: (tr) The Granger Collection; (bl) The Granger Collection. 169: (tr) Flip Schulke/CORBIS; (bl) The Granger Collection; (br) The Granger Collection. 174: (bl) (inset) George Wright. 175: (b) Compliments of Kings County Library; (cr) Renee Knoeber/AP-WideWorld. 180: (tr) (br) Rib Lake Plywood, Inc.